W. T Pratt

Colonial Experiences

Incidents and Reminiscences of Thirty-Four Years in New Zealand

W. T Pratt

Colonial Experiences

Incidents and Reminiscences of Thirty-Four Years in New Zealand

ISBN/EAN: 9783337154707

Printed in Europe, USA, Canada, Australia, Japan

Cover: Foto ©Suzi / pixelio.de

More available books at **www.hansebooks.com**

COLONIAL EXPERIENCES:

OR,

INCIDENTS AND REMINISCENCES

OF

THIRTY-FOUR YEARS IN NEW ZEALAND.

BY

AN OLD COLONIST.

> "Hear, Land o' Cakes, and brither Scots,
> Frae Maidenkirk to Johnny Groat's;
> If there's a hole in a' your coats,
>   I rede you tent it:
> A chield's amang you, taking notes,
>   And, faith, he'll prent it."—*Burns.*

LONDON:
CHAPMAN & HALL, 193, PICCADILLY.
1877.

Dedication

To the Hon. W. Fox, M.A., Late Premier
of New Zealand.

Sir,—As one of the pioneers of colonization in New Zealand, with whose social and political progress you have been identified through a long course of years, this personal experience of an old Colonist is, with kind permission, respectfully inscribed by

THE AUTHOR.

CHRISTCHURCH, CANTERBURY, NEW ZEALAND,
February, 1877.

INTRODUCTION.

It is the peculiar privilege of an author to have the first and last word. In virtue of the former, I desire to make a few remarks, premising that they will be brief and to the point.

It is nearly forty years since the systematic colonization of New Zealand was commenced. The ranks of the earlier settlers are rapidly thinning, and a new generation of workers are occupying their places; to whom an epitome of the early days, written by one of the former, may possess special interest, albeit the writer may be without either literary ability or experience.

It is generally admitted that colonists do not often rush into print; they are either too busy, or the constant strain, and physical exertions of colonial life, indispose to literary efforts; from whatever cause, there is a dearth of works relating exclusively to the colonies, written by colonists.

The writer of the following sketches has no pretentions towards supplying this want, but ventures to hope this humble attempt to produce a picture from his limited standpoint, of a primitive state of things now passed away, will be received with liberal allowances for its many faults and crudities.

And that it may also merit a kind consideration and support from a large and widening circle interested in the progress and advancement of "England's Colonial Empire," is the sincerest wish of the

AUTHOR.

CONTENTS.

CHAP.		PAGE
I.	RETROSPECTIVE AND DISCURSIVE	1
II.	A STEP DOWNWARD	33
III.	DISCARDED	54
IV.	ARCADIAN	69
V.	HARD LINES	96
VI.	A FRESH START	109
VII.	DECIDEDLY NAUTICAL	154
VIII.	DOWN SOUTH	175
IX.	A STEP UPWARD.	199
X.	A STEP MATRIMONIAL	238
XI.	TRULY RURAL	249
XII.	IN HARNESS AGAIN	273
XIII.	RETIREMENT	282
XIV.	CONCLUDING REMARKS	284

COLONIAL EXPERIENCES.

CHAPTER I.

RETROSPECTIVE AND DISCURSIVE.

AFTER an uneventful passage of 125 days the welcome cry of land O! was heard on board the ship Indus, 420 tons, McKenzie master, bound from London to the at that time recently formed settlement of Nelson, New Zealand.

It was Saturday morning, February 4th, 1843, when this heart-stirring sound sent an electric thrill of expectation and delight through the whole ship's company, galvanizing into sudden activity nerves and susceptibilities rendered almost torpid by the comparative confinement and monotony of a four months' voyage. Though

B

such a voyage would be deemed a long one now, and seemed long enough to the voyagers, yet in point of time it was considered a fair average one in those early trips to the antipodes.

During the night Cape Farewell was rounded, and on Sunday—a beautifully fine summer day, conveying a pleasing assurance of the salubrity of the climate—we were sailing pleasantly along in smooth water with a light wind down Blind Bay. About 4 o'clock a boat was observed approaching with two occupants; on coming alongside, I learnt that one was Captain Moore, and his companion a Maori waihine or native woman, who remained in the boat nursing a cat. This was my first introduction to an aboriginal, and a very comely specimen she appeared, notwithstanding the partial disfigurement of the tattooing. The ship was brought to an anchor shortly afterwards off the Boulder Bank, the tide not suiting to enter the harbour until 10 A.M. next day. There were great numbers of dogfish disporting round the vessel, and many of the passengers amused themselves by capturing them. Next morning, just at break of day, I was startled by hearing the crow of a cock on shore; it was so unexpected as, so far, no houses had been seen, the township not being visible from where the vessel lay at anchor. Anchored in that calm bay, in the quiet of the early morn, with no perceptible movement of the ship, and no sound save the gentle lapping of the water at the side, as with the strong ebb-tide it rippled and gurgled by the ship, it seemed as if the peace of Heaven had suddenly fallen around and upon us; the reaction was so great after the perpetual unrest—the continuous heaving, and surging, and creaking of the labouring vessel, to which we had been subjected the past four months; it was like entering upon a new existence. I hastily dressed and hurried on deck, having made an appointment to witness the first sun-rise upon this prospective new home. As day advanced, wreaths of vapoury mist rolled majestically away, detached fragments like a beaten host lingering in the valleys until finally dispersed, while the lofty peaks of neighbouring hills caught the golden flush of the rising sun.

Gradually the golden flood descended the hill-sides, lighting up the valleys; the blending light and shade causing the varied ridges and low points to stand out sharply defined in the cool clear morning air. Though several years have passed away since then, I never hear the shrill clarion of the cock at morn, but the whole scene and its sweetly tender associations are brought vividly to my remembrance in all their former freshness and beauty. And then the hearing at such a time and place that old familiar sound, with its human associations, on this otherwise apparently desolate shore, giving evidence of English homes, and all that is comprised in that word, but cannot be expressed, was sufficient to profoundly stir sympathies especially attuned to such influences by the recent abrupt severance of all old ties, and the subsequent irksomeness of a protracted voyage. And by my side was one who shared my sentiments and feelings, and whose mind I had long learnt to lovingly regard as the counterpart and reflex of my own—for by pre-arrangement we had romantically agreed to witness together the rising sun shine for the first time for us upon our adopted country, our future home.

And hand in hand we gazed upon this new world opening out before us, feeling in leaving the old one a new and exquisite sense of freedom in the present, and a trustful faith in the future, that forcibly contrasted with the trials and difficulties that had sorely oppressed us, and that appeared at one time almost insurmountable and from which we appeared to have miraculously escaped. To us the glad vista of the future assumed all the roseate hues of the opening day, which with hearts too full for converse we were silently absorbed in witnessing, and deeming its splendour in some way prophetic of our future happiness.

Alas! that hopes so bright and promising should soon prove so fleeting and delusive; ere many months had passed the hand then fondly clasped in mine was given to another, and as his bride she sailed gaily away to old England, bidding, it was supposed, a final adieu to New

Zealand. And yet a few brief years saw her returned with a widowed heart, and for many years the grass has grown green above her, upon one of those sunlit points that we were all unconsciously gazing upon that summer morning, thirty four years ago.

O Time! thou avenger and maturer of all things; trials, and their compensations; whose effacing fingers soften and obliterate the sharply chiselled lines on the marble, sacred to the memory of the loved one; by whose benignant and consoling power, griefs, that appear to overwhelm, are succeeded by new joys; and regrets and tears are comparatively transient when measured by the truer standard of life's possibilities.

In thus gently lifting the veil that has so long enshrouded the episode in my life, I have somewhat anticipated the sequence of events; but will resume my experiences as far as my memory will permit in the due order of their occurrence.

On Monday morning, February 6, the 'Indus' was piloted to a berth inside the Boulder Bank, passing in her course the hull of the

'Fifeshire,' a wreck fast upon a ledge of rocks upon which she had been swept by the strong current, while attempting to leave the harbour at a dangerous state of the tide, then not sufficiently known.

I and others were landed on the beach from a boat that we were sure was the private property of the pilot, as his wife in no very choice language soundly rated the boatmen in charge for allowing its keel to grate on the stones, which with a kindly desire to lessen the discomfort of their passengers having to wade on shore, they had endeavoured to approach as near as possible, but even then, the boat being large and heavily laden, and drawing a good deal of water, it left a margin of several yards to be waded through. The boatmen very gallantly carried the females ashore, but the men had to jump out; and I, happening to alight upon a treacherous boulder, fell prone, and, like an illustrious namesake of old, thus took fief of the new land.

The family with whom I had immigrated consisted of a Mr. E——, his wife and three daughters. There was a large quantity of luggage, and considerable difficulty was experienced in removing it from the landing-place to the immigration depot, at a distance of about two miles, as there were no carriers or carts available for this purpose. After some delay a hand truck was procured, and I may truthfully say my first essay at real hard work was assisting to remove that luggage to its destination.

The road was newly made, and, from the absence of wheeled vehicles, very rough; my wellington boots very thin, and soddened with sea-water, my hands and muscles very soft; and, moreover, the temperature was about 95° in the shade, and the intense glare of the sun being reflected from the white road, made the heat almost insupportable. E. took the lead with the truck, while I laboured behind. Not having expected a job of this kind, I had landed in holiday costume, under a vague impression that it was, or ought to be, a sort of gala day; and my position in the rear of that truck, wearing a black cloth cut-away coat, and a "bell-topper" must have been exceedingly picturesque and amusing to the onlookers, as indeed their broad grins abundantly testified during our progress along the road. E. was a shipwright and boat-builder, and it had been arranged that I was to work with him with the object of learning his business. After the preceding remarks, I need not add that my love for his eldest daughter was the irresistible impulse that had impelled me to follow the fortunes of the family to New Zealand, and to throw in my lot with them, and, like Jacob of old, I was only too happy to work and wait for my Rachael.

A few days after arrival at the depot, E. received an order to build a boat, which rendered it necessary to look out for a suitable house or shed in the vicinity of the tide-way. One was bought for I believe five pounds, which was considered a great bargain, combining as it did the advantages of size and site. It was bought from a Pakeha Maori, one who had lived a long time with Maories, until he had become almost naturalized.

The house had been probably built by Maories, as it closely resembled the houses in their pahs, and being situate where their canoes could approach very near, had evidently been a place of frequent resort by them. I suspect it was this fact and other supposed belongings that was the secret of its being sold so cheap. It was thatched with raupo, or native bulrush, and had sides and interior partitions of the same material. That night I carried some blankets down to sleep there, as it had been decided to make certain alterations before the family removed into it.

I had not retired to rest long when I began to experience some extraordinary and unaccountable sensations; tingling all over with a supposed rash, I nervously longed for daylight to solve the mystery; and the solution was very far from satisfactory; the place swarmed with myriads of fleas of the most active and industrious order, a race peculiar, I afterwards learnt, to Maori pahs. I seized my clothes and blankets, and after giving them a good shaking in the open air, rushed incontinently into the creek close by, as the readiest way of getting relief, and eluding my tormentors.

On reporting the state of affairs it was decided to remove the interior partitions, to well water and sweep the floor, which not being boarded, had a layer of two or three inches of dry earth trodden into impalpable dust, and to line the inside of the rush walls at one end of the shed with blue clay that was close at hand, and by laying down a floor of concrete composed of lime, sand, and fine gravel, we hoped to get rid of the pest, and render one part at least habitable—the remainder being required for a workshop. This was accomplished in a few days, and the family and effects removed into it.

As families were only allowed to remain a limited time at the depot, houses had to be procured somehow, and they were improvised in many instances after a very peculiar fashion, and in such variety that it would be almost impossible to attempt to describe them.

Fern about two feet high still covered the greater part of the township, small clearings being made round the homesteads to protect them from fire, and the roads, with the exception of the two main streets, were merely tracks cut or trodden through the fern. In some instances the fern was used for closing in the sides and even roofs of shanties.

I was passing one of this description one day situate on low land near the river, and ventured to express an opinion that fern thatch could not afford much protection from rain, and that I thought some danger was to be apprehended from the rising of the river, when the matron of the house replied : " Oh ! the river often rises, and the rain pours through the roof, and then we stand on the top of a big box, and hold up an umbrella all night," and this was said with a tone and manner as if it was the most natural thing in the world to do, and really all that was possible under the circumstances.

Those whose means enabled them to procure timber, and employ carpenters, came out in all the glories of a weather-boarded building in the prevailing style, a door and two windows in front, a lean-to behind, and the luxury of a brick chimney. But sod chimneys were the rule, brick ones the exception, some contenting themselves with little more than the fire-place only. I remember an amusing incident connected with one of these low chimneys that is worth narrating here. A young fellow, a single man, who shared a small wharé, with another robust youth like himself, full of fun and practical jokes, was strolling round one Sunday morning when his attention was attracted by a very appetising flavour proceeding from the low chimney of a neighbour, a young simple-minded bachelor, who was often made a victim of practical jokes.

A. at once confided to his mate Joe, his opinion that so-and-so, whom we will call B. was roasting a duck for dinner, and they forthwith devised a scheme to possess it.

Joe provided himself with a piece of hoop-iron turned up at one end to form a hook, and a fork securely fastened to a stick, both being about three feet in length.

A. then sauntered leisurely round to the front of the house where the duck was roasting, and engaged the amateur cook in conversation, meanwhile Joe, leaning over the low wall of the fire-place, with the hook quietly raised the lid of the camp oven hanging over the fire, then dexterously inserted the fork, and the duck was won. When A. was satisfied that Joe had effected a masterly retreat, he took out his pipe and walked in towards the fireplace to light it, and was in the act of retiring again when he heard a hurried exclamation of "By Jove, the duck!" and B. rushed past him, and to the rear of the house, and after gazing vacantly round returned very much concerned for the loss of his dinner, vowing vengeance against the delinquent. A. condoled with him in his loss, and said that Joe had snared a duck that morning, and *generously* invited him to come and share it with them, and having slily noticed some potatoes in the camp oven looking nice and brown, added, "By the bye, we haven't got any potatoes, so you had better bring these along and we'll make a jolly good dinner." Joe had so manipulated the duck that there was no suspicion. Dinner disposed of, pipes alight, and conversation brisk, B. remarked that as powder and shot was expensive he would like Joe to show him how he snared ducks; Joe, with a knowing smile, produced the hoop-iron time it seemed endowed with the power of a galvanic battery, judging by the shocks communicated to my arms and shoulders. After spending some time in a vain endeavour to control its vagaries, E. sent me to the sawyers with his compliments and the saw, I feeling at the time that I had sunk immeasurably in his opinion of my capacity and usefulness.

This was an unfortunate commencement of my new occupation, but I soon acquired fair skill in the use of the tools, and being actuated by a strong desire to learn and make myself a necessity in the business, matters progressed very fairly, I even winning occasional commendations from E.

The boat was finished in good time, and its spirited owner gave a supper to a select party of friends upon the occasion of the launch and christening, to which we were invited; one of the most genial and hilarious of the guests, named McGregor, was shortly after numbered with the victims slain by the Maories in the massacre at the Wairau. The building of another and larger boat, suitable for trading

C

across the bay was next undertaken for a Mr. H., a young man, a fellow-passenger in the 'Indus.'

At the same time arrangements were made by the E.'s to admit him as a lodger, and then commenced the insidious advances that resulted in his supplanting me in the affections of the girl for whose sake I had left home, friends, and country to come sixteen thousand miles to win and wed.

Turning for a time from purely personal matters, it will be of more general interest to refer to the social and political prospects of the young settlement at this time, which I shall endeavour to do as far as my humble ability and limited opportunities for observation will permit.

The first anniversary of the founding of the settlement had come and gone, and considering the backward state of the surveys, owing to the natural and physical difficulties of the country to be surveyed, and the disadvantages of the system adopted for the choice of sections, it was not surprising that at this time only about half-a-dozen enterprising men had begun farming operations at the Waimea.

It was generally admitted that the system of deciding orders of choice by a species of lottery in England, had resulted even at that early date in retarding settlement, and in many other ways to its great detriment; and it required all the energy and tact of the resident agent, Captain Wakefield, to devise remedial measures to avert the total collapse and failure of the settlement.

To encourage farming operations, and show the fertility of the soil, he had established a model farm at the Waimea, which was well managed, and the experience gained was doubtless of great advantage to new comers contemplating entering into farming pursuits. Very little attention was paid at this time to pastoral matters.

This may have been owing to the absence of the Australian element that was subsequently so favourable to the Canterbury Settlement, but more particularly from the infrequent communication with the Australian colonies. Enormous prices had been paid per head for the few cattle and horses in the settlement, working bullocks were about £30 each, and cows £50, and a carter, I knew well, paid £110 for an ordinary carthorse, and for a long time his was the only horse and cart in the town available for general carting work.

Salt and fresh pork were plentiful, but mutton only occasionally procurable, and then at 1s. per lb. Bread was reasonable, being sold at 1s. the four-pound loaf, but this was entirely due to the Company's agent keeping a vessel especially chartered to go to Valparaiso for flour, and retailing the same at the Company's store at 20s. per hundred pound's weight; butter 2s. 6d., and milk too scarce to enter into general consumption. Groceries and ordinary stores at very moderate prices for so young a settlement.

At this time nearly all the labouring population were in the employ of the Company, forming and making roads, and with the exception of a few families located at Motueka and Riwaka on the opposite side of the bay, were concentrated in and about the township, entirely dependent upon the Company employment; and to show its eleemosynary character, married men with families were paid according to one scale, and single men another and lower rate, while each class was expected to execute the same amount of work. It was well-known the Company's labour expenditure could not be long continued, and reductions and fresh regulations were frequently being made, with the object of forcing the men to find other employment, but with only partial success. Those who had commenced farming, having been accustomed to the scale of wages prevailing in the agricultural districts of England, were not disposed to give even as much as the Company, otherwise I think they would have attracted all the labour they required. The scale of payment for married men was 14s. per week and 10 lb. rations, and single men 14s. per week and 7 lb. rations, the ration in each case being 10 lb. meat and 10 lb. flour, and 7 lb. meat and 7 lb. flour, with tea and sugar in proportion.

The pressure brought to bear upon the

Company's agent by the land purchasers, to still further reduce the scale, acquired for them a degree of unpopularity that was long remembered, and manifested itself upon the occasion of some memorable elections that afterwards took place upon the introduction of constitutional government. Unfortunately for the future welfare of the settlement that was not the only occasion upon which the class feeling, and antagonism engendered by the proceedings referred to, had an opportunity of displaying itself, and which I shall refer to again when treating of the compensation claims.

Some amusing scenes sometimes occurred at the attempted reductions referred to; upon the men being informed that the wages at the next pay-day would be so much less than hitherto, they would quietly smile at the information, and proceed to their work as usual, feeling confident their cause was in good hands. And when Saturday noon, the paytime, arrived, the men's wives would muster about 200 strong, and in true Amazonian style, march in a body down the beach to the pay-office at the port, and sturdily refusing to submit to any reductions, keep up such a clamour that the officials, after sustaining a two or three hours' siege, would receive orders to pay the old rate, and matters would go on again in their old groove until the next fit of retrenchment came on, when a similar scene would be enacted and generally with the same result. In a settlement like Canterbury, with an almost unlimited extent of level land of good average quality, such a system of allotment as was adopted for the selection of land in Nelson, would have given general dissatisfaction to the land purchasers, and imperilled the success of the settlement; and it may be readily imagined how the evil was intensified in Nelson, when the hilly character of the country and limited extent of agricultural land are considered; disadvantages that would not present themselves to the land purchaser until his arrival in the colony, and there is no doubt had the effect of sending many away in disgust, possessing both capital and energy, who would have proved good settlers.

Fancy the disappointment and chagrin of a small farmer who had expended nearly all his capital in the purchase of one or more sections of land, and embarked with his family, resolved to carve out for himself a new home; finding upon his arrival in the colony that his land was situated upon the top of some inaccessible mountain, or in an impossible-to-be-drained swamp, or on the extreme boundaries of the settlement, so remote that in the absence of roads it might as well be in the moon.

I have known of young men with fair prospects, possessing moderate but sufficient means to make a fair start in life, had no impediment existed to their at once occupying their lands, remaining about the township, dissipating their means, and acquiring habits of intemperance that must have seriously damaged their future prospects, if no worse result followed such indulgencies.

One spirited land purchaser upon finding it was physically impossible to put him in possession of the land he had purchased, forthwith returned to England and brought an action for damages against the New Zealand Company, and the matter was compromised by the Company paying him £900 I believe.

Upon the Company learning it was the opinion of their legal adviser that they were liable to a series of actions of the same kind, they resolved to compensate all the resident land purchasers by allowing them to select from the unsold lands, so much extra land in proportion to their original purchases.

This was both just and politic, and, although too late to remedy all the mischief entailed upon individuals and the settlement, would have been of far greater advantage to the latter had it not been for the intemperate and short-sighted action of one man of the "parlour orator" type, so aptly described by Charles Dickens.

This individual got up an agitation in Nelson in favour of the absentee land purchasers, that (meeting with special favour in high quarters) not only neutralised many of the advantages of the previous measure, but inflicted untold injury upon the settlement, and was mainly answerable for its subsequent depressed condition.

This man had a morbid dislike to the resident land purchasers, whom he was in the habit of designating "land sharks"; and anything calculated to benefit them had the same exciting effect upon him as the red flag is supposed to have upon an enraged bull, and when the compensation scheme was made known in the settlement, he convened a public meeting, and having numerous followers for reasons previously referred to, was enabled to carry a string of resolutions recommending compensation to the absentee land purchasers, insanely supposing that by such action he was spiting the resident land purchaser.

These resolutions were duly forwarded to the Governor, Sir G. Grey, who upon this occasion exhibited a remarkable deference to *public opinion* by immediately passing an ordinance in council authorising the issue of an almost unlimited quantity of scrip to the absentees, who, having no grievance, must have been wonderfully elated at such unwonted liberality.

There was a whisper of a certain gentleman, who was in the colony upon a visit at the time, receiving a large quantity of the said scrip, in his character of an absentee land purchaser, and with it becoming the almost sole proprietor of a small province not far from Wellington.

But for the miserably insignificant croakings of a few imbeciles affording a colourable pretext, even Sir G. Grey, arbitrary and despotic as he showed himself at that time, would scarcely have ventured the introduction and passing of such a measure. It was universally denounced in the colony, and was considered in England of such a questionable character, and so detrimental to the colony's interests, that the Queen's assent was withheld, notwithstanding which it was put in force, and the scrip issued.

Sir G. Grey's recent utterances in the House, in the debate on the Abolition Bill, and supporting his opposition to its coming into force upon the grounds of its not having been submitted to the Law Officers of the Crown, or received the Queen's assent, displays a new found reverence for Imperial authority, in strong contrast to his former action connected with the " absentee script ordinance."

By a singular Nemesis, the individual who had been chiefly instrumental in bringing this infliction and loss upon the settlement was twice elected to fill the highest position in the province (a sufficient leaven of the old feeling remaining to secure this result), a position of all others where the impoverished state of the finances, resulting from the extinction of so much land scrip, would most obtrude upon his notice, and he must have been obtuse indeed, if he did not then feel the full extent of the mischief which his paltry gratification of class feeling had brought upon the province.

It is worthy of remark that at the time of the issuing of this scrip, the price of the crown lands of the colony was twenty shillings per acre, and the scrip was of the nominal value of twenty shillings and representing one acre; but some time afterwards, when by the fiat of Sir George, the price of all the unsold land in the colony, except the Canterbury block, was by proclamation reduced to five and ten shillings per acre, the original nominal value of the scrip was insisted on by the holders, when paying for land at the reduced price, so that scrip originally representing one acre, was passed into the treasury in payment of two or four acres, according to the class of land applied for—so that for all the unextinguished scrip by the reduction in the price of land, the original evil was doubled, and quadrupled.

Nearly all the unsold available land in the Nelson province was paid for in scrip, thus leaving it without a land fund for the prosecution of public works.

It was not alone the scrip issued to the Nelson absentees, but also a large portion issued to the Wellington land purchasers, that Nelson was called upon to extinguish.

When, by what is known as the Compact of 1856, Nelson, Canterbury, and Otago, undertook the liquidation of the New Zealand Company's debt of £200,000, and having sole control of their land fund, each to become liable for one third of the amount, in a subsequent session of the General Assembly Sir David Munro advocated the justice of relieving Nelson of a considerable share of the burden, on the grounds that the province had been and was still specially weighted with the extinguishing of nearly all the compensation scrip issued in the colony.

It was well known at the time of the reduction of the price of the land that a Nelson land agent was the holder of about £40,000 worth of this scrip, and his standing advertisement in the 'Nelson Examiner' to intending land purchasers, by offering certain terms of credit, had the effect of intercepting nearly every pound that would have otherwise found its way to the Waste-lands Board; he, the agent, allowing the purchaser to select the land wanted, and himself paying the Government for it in scrip.

The boat which I have left so long on the stocks was finished and launched in due course, and no further orders coming in, matters began to assume an ominous aspect, as although our living was arranged upon a very frugal scale, even that involved a certain weekly expenditure for which a corresponding income was indispensable.

To show that it was not of a very luxurious

character, but, in the words of a Paris restaurant keeper, both " fortifying and simple," I subjoin a few details, which will be fairly descriptive of the style of living that generally prevailed at this time.

Bread, no butter or milk, salt pork, occasionally a joint of fresh pork for a change, potatoes, tea and coffee sweetened with very dark Mauritius sugar, and to vary the fare sometimes, a kind of rice stew, made by boiling with rice a small quantity of fresh pork, cut into small pieces and suitable seasoning added.

The salt pork was American barrelled, very prime to look at, but possessing the remarkable property of almost vanishing in the pot, and reappearing again upon the cooling of the water in which it had been boiled in the shape of a two-inch cake of fat.

Potatoes were procurable from the Maories in flax kits, at from one to five shillings the kit, which estimated by weight would be at the rate of about £6 the ton.

They were also the purveyors of the fresh pork sold by the butchers.

Pigs with such extraordinary long snouts I am sure were never seen out of New Zealand. They were peculiarly well adapted for rooting up fern root, their staple food, and afforded a good illustration of Darwin's theory of the "survival of the fittest," as it might be fairly concluded that all the short-nosed pigs had perished in the struggle for existence.

On Sundays, in honour of the day, and to preserve an ancient tradition of puddings of some kind or other having graced former dinners in the old country, in addition to the ordinary fare, an apple-pudding was improvised out of a pumpkin; which was done by cutting a portion of a pumpkin into small pieces, and making and cooking it in the same manner as an apple-pudding; and with the addition of a small quantity of tartaric acid we used to *make* believe it tasted exactly like one.

CHAPTER II.

A STEP DOWNWARD.

AFTER a brief period of enforced idleness, or rather of odd jobs about the house that brought no return, I suggested to E. the expediency of my applying to the Company's agent for work on the roads, until more work in the boat-building line offered, as at this time the weekly wages paid to single men was 18s. without rations. The family strongly objected, as with their English notions they could not disabuse their minds of the idea of such employment being derogatory; but I, feeling their objections were entirely unselfish, and advanced solely on my account, they not wishing me to engage in such new and uncongenial employment, thought it my duty to be firm, as no other means offered by which I could avoid being a burden upon them, and at the same time, in a small degree, assist the house expenses. To lessen the unpleasantness I knew this resolve would cause them if I were employed anywhere in the neighbourhood, I applied to be sent to a working party engaged about eight miles from town.

This involved an enforced banishment from the house, from very early on Monday morning until the following Saturday afternoon, which at that time was to me by far the severest part of the undertaking, as it left the course clear for the machinations of my rival, whose designs I intuitively began to suspect.

Matters being all arranged, and with a thick rug, and a week's supply of provisions, consisting of two home-baked loaves about 5 lbs. each, 7 lb. piece of salt pork (cooked), some tea and sugar, and a small tin can for making tea in, the whole compactly stowed in a Maori kit, and carried on the back with Maori flax-made slings, like a soldier's knapsack, I started about 4 o'clock on Monday morning for the scene of my new employment.

And thus ended my boat-building career, for circumstances soon occurred that effectually prevented any future resumption of that employment. A considerable part of the road I had to travel lay across mud-flats covered by the tide at high water, and into which I sank over my boots at each step, and occasionally to the knees in crossing the numerous water-courses that intersected the flats.

Arrived at the scene of operations, wet and weary from the difficulties of the road and the load carried, I found the party of men with whom I was to work numbered sixteen including myself, besides an overseer or ganger to direct operations.

The work consisted in cutting a siding road round the base of hills washed by the tide at high water. Only two or three of the men appeared to me to be of the regular navvy type, the rest like myself had not been accustomed to this kind of work.

The habitation to which the party retired, upon the conclusion of the day's work at 5 o'clock, had been formed by digging into the side of the hill in a small gully, thus forming three sides of the house, while the fourth side or front being the lowest, was built up with sods, the roof thatched with toi-toi, and sloping from the highest part of the cutting to the front wall, following the slope of the hill so nearly that it was almost invisible at a short distance.

In the back wall a fireplace was excavated, and a shaft sunk to it from the hill above, which formed an excellent chimney, and on either side wide benches of the earth had been left when excavating, about two feet in height and extending the width of the house from front to back; upon this a thick layer of New Zealand feathers (dried fern) was laid and formed the sleeping quarters of the inmates.

I suspect it was due to the presence of the navvies that such a compact and comfortable residence had been provided.

Brief as my colonial experience had been at this time, I had become accustomed to many things that were new and strange, and in some instances not altogether to my taste or inclinations, and simply from a desire to make the best of what could not be altered or avoided; but when I saw the sleeping accommodation I instinctively recoiled from such a communistic arrangement.

As soon as tea was disposed of, I set about the construction of a bedstead in a spare corner of the appartment.

In the immediate neighbourhood was a wooded gully from which I procured six forked stakes about 30 inches in length; these, when driven into the ground at suitable distances and at a uniform height, to form the framework, received the side-pieces in the forks, and by lacing it across with broad leaves of flax, a very easy and comfortable couch was provided that quite excited the envy of my companions.

Occasionally I experienced the incovenience of a break-down in the night, when the flax got dry and tender.

I remember that at this time I was gifted with an enormous appetite, which might under he circumstances be deemed a very questionable advantage ; I know it required some self-denial to make my provisions last their appointed time. Working in the open air, and the very fact of having to allowance the consumption of each meal, there is no doubt tended to increase a desire that never seemed thoroughly appeased.

I was not singular in this respect, for generally by Saturday morning, there was not among the whole party, more than would have sufficed for a tolerable breakfast for one.

One Friday morning at breakfast time the overseer wishing to have a certain piece of road completed that week, offered the men the opportunity of finishing it as quickly as they liked for their week's work.

The offer was cheerfully accepted as we judged the work could be done in time to allow of our starting to town soon after noon. Upon the faith of accomplishing this there was a general consumption of the then remaining provisions at that breakfast without causing any very alarming symptoms from repletion.

The contract was finished by two o'clock; having worked hard and continuously from eight including our dinner hour, as having no dinner to dispose of, it was unnecessary to stop the usual hour.

As we were conveying the barrows and tools in the direction of our wharé we were met by the Superintendent of Road who naturally enquired where we were going. The overseer could not explain the little contract he had made, so replied that we were going to lessen some of the abrupt curves in another part of the road; consequently instead of proceeding to the wharé, and preparing for a start home, we were, to save the credit of the overseer, reluctantly obliged to set to work upon the part of the road he had indicated, until the superintendent returned from a visit he was making to a Mr. Jollie, some distance beyond the work upon which we were engaged.

He did not return until nearly five o'clock, and it being then almost dark, and too late to start for town, we retired to our wharé in no very enviable state of mind or stomach. Next morning we started to town minus a breakfast.

Arriving about 11 o'clock I walked into the

first small store I came to, and after disposing of a two-pound loaf and half a pound of butter, felt in capital trim for my dinner to which I shortly after did ample justice. I had not been many weeks at this work when news was brought to Nelson of the massacre at the Wairau.

It created a general feeling of insecurity and alarm, and heartfelt regret for the victims of this savage onslaught, among whom were many of the leading gentlemen of the settlement.

Being so near the scene of the tragedy, it was considered that the savage instincts of the natives having been excited and emboldened by success, they would probably attack the township; energetic measures were therefore made to meet such a contingency. Nearly all the adult males in the town and vicinity were enrolled, armed, and drilled, the hill in the centre of the town now crowned with a church was scarped and bastioned, and a considerable area on its summit enclosed with thick planks looped-holed for musketry, into which it was intended the women and children should retreat if the town was attacked. It was judged

A Step Downward.

that any attempted attack would be by the natives approaching stealthily in the night, and for which the bay, at or near where the shore end of the Australian cable is now landed, and an inland valley leading from it, offered great facilities for their getting very near the town unobserved. It was therefore deemed important to have a watch upon this part of the coast.

The road party that I had recently joined was constituted the watch, and we were sworn special constables, our duties being to keep a vigilant watch upon the bay by day, and the inland opening of the valley by night, until recalled; and to signal to the town, distant about nine miles, anything portentous by lighting a signal fire upon a lofty peak upon which we had collected a large quantity of firewood, dried fern, etc. I think we had been engaged upon this duty nearly three weeks, when news reached Nelson that Rauparaha and his party had crossed Cook's Straits, and the watch was withdrawn.

During this period there was no panic, but a cool and firm resolve to make a determined stand against the expected assailants, however numerous and savage they might prove, and only such precautionary measures were adopted as circumstances appeared to render necessary and judicious.

The friendly natives living at the Motueka, on the opposite side of the bay, were in great fear lest they should be held accountable, and made to suffer for the doings at the Wairau, as in accordance with their savage notions such reprisals were usual and customary among the various tribes of native inhabitants.

It required considerable tact and exertions on the part of those having influence over them to allay their fears and convince them of the more just and humane policy of the Europeans.

It may not be out of place to notice here an occurrence prior to, but closely connected with this tragic event, as in none of the accounts published has any reference been made to it that I am aware of.

Some time in the month of February, 1843, Rauparaha and Ranghiaita and a numerous following visited Nelson and had a long and

A Step Downward. 43

angry korero with Captain Wakefield respecting the land at the Wairau, maintaining that it had not been included in the land sold to Wide-awake (Col. Wakefield) for the new settlement (Nelson) and threatening to mati moi (kill or tomahawk) any one going there to put in the rakau (wood, meaning the surveyor's pegs).

Captain Wakefield regarded these threats as mere native bravado, and having entertained them for two or three days, by distributing a quantity of flour and sugar among them, and their departing in exuberant spirits, apparently well pleased with their reception, he concluded that having got all he supposed they came for, namely, a good feed, no more would be heard of these absurd claims.

This, be it remarked, was the first introduction of the flour and sugar policy, and how lamentably it failed upon this occasion to " soothe the savage breast" subsequent events only too sadly showed.

When Rauparaha heard the surveyors were at work at the Wairau, he re-crossed the Straits with a strong party and ordered them to leave, at the same time pulling down the tents, and firing the huts. Upon these proceedings being reported to Captain Wakefield, he thought all that was necessary was to make a display of force, to at once overawe a parcel of savages; and as the Government brig happened to be in the harbour at the time, he took the opportunity to assemble, and convey to the mouth of the Wairau river, in Cloudy bay, about 20 men from a road party working on the beach road. These were each supplied from the Company's store with an old Tower musket with flint lock, being part of the stock used in barter with the natives for their land; muskets, powder, and blankets were the chief articles of exchange, as being in great request, and most highly prized by the Maories. Many of the men had never handled fire-arms before, and so little did Captain Wakefield think of any necessity arising for their use that no instructions, it appears, were given even in the simple matter of loading them, as it was well known that several of the muskets were afterwards found loaded with the ball-end of the cartridge downwards.

So weak and inefficient a force was totally unfitted to cope with such redoubtable fighting chiefs as Rauparaha and Ranghiaita and their numerous followers, well trained in many a desperate encounter with neighbouring tribes.

Several gentlemen volunteered to join the expedition; and to give it a legal colouring, a warrant for the apprehension of Rauparaha for arson was issued by Mr. Thompson, the resident magistrate, who with Malin, the chief constable, accompanied the expedition to execute it.

The sad catastrophe that followed is only too well known. After shots had been exchanged and several wounded on either side, Captain Wakefield, who with some of the gentlemen had become separated from the remainder of the party through a little delay in re-crossing the river, was anxious to unite his forces on the rising ground a short distance from the river; but part of the guard on retiring for this purpose continued their retreat up the hill, gradually accelerating their speed, disregarding Captain Wakefield's orders and entreaties to stop. After following them for a short distance, Captain Wakefield, the gentlemen, and a few of the guard that had remained together with him, halted on the side of the hill, and faced about to the Maories, at the same time holding up his white handkerchief as a signal for a cessation of firing. The natives immediately rushed up the hill to where they had halted, Ranghiaita stopping on the way to tomahawk those who had fallen on the hill side wounded. Mr. Cotterill, one of the surveyors, had halted before Captain Wakefield and his companions, and was sitting down on the slope, about half way between his own party and the Maoris, coolly filling his pipe, when he was brutally despatched. The natives disdained to follow the fugitives up the hill, having got all the Rangitiras in their power. What followed was told me by an eye-witness, who surrendered with the rest, and escaped by a miracle almost, and was for some time working in the same road party as myself. His name was Bamford, and while the Maori who was mounting guard over him had his attention absorbed in watching the

A Step Downward. 47

sanguinary scene that was being enacted, he quietly slid into the high fern, and creeping a short distance down towards the gully, fortunately remained undiscovered.

On surrounding the party, and taking possession of their arms, an attempt was made to take off Captain Wakefield's coat; this he resented by snapping a pistol at the offender, but it missed fire. Mr. Howard, who was standing near, said, " For God's sake, Captain, be calm, don't excite them." The natives, far outnumbering their prisoners, then contrived to isolate them by insinuating themselves between them, and Ranghiaita nimbly stepping behind each in turn, his tomahawk did its deadly work.

I was working for some time in company with one of the party who accompanied the Rev. Mr. Ironsides from Queen Charlotte Sound to the scene of the massacre, a few days after its occurrence, to inter the bodies of the unfortunate victims. He told me it was a ghastly sight; Brooks the interpreter could only be recognised by his clothes. They appeared to have wreaked special vengeance upon him as there were no distinguishable features remaining; and with savage irony they had placed a damper (flour cake) under Captain Wakefield's head, and laid his pistol across his throat. The threat made four months previously had been only too literally fulfilled.

Considering the weakness and isolation at that time of the two small settlements of Wellington and Nelson, it would not have been politic, nor indeed practicable, to have attempted the arrest of the perpetrators of these savage murders, as they had retired to their stronghold; but on the other hand, the attitude of Governor Fitzroy and the two Clarks, father and son, called the Protectors of "Aborigines" forsooth! in not alone condemning the proceedings of the settlers, but in a manner justifying the actions of the natives in this affair, was an outrage upon the sympathies and common sense of the entire community; knowing what a pernicious effect was likely to be produced upon the native mind, by the publicly notified approval of their actions by the Governor. The result was soon apparent, as the astute Maori, construing the impunity for the past as evidence of fear and weakness, made a raid upon the settlers in the Hult Valley, near Wellington, and many valuable lives were lost before they were finally quelled. At the time the New Zealand Company began the colonization of these islands, there arose an influential party at home, distinguished as the "Exeter Hall Party," whose sympathies were enlisted on behalf of the native inhabitants, whom they were instructed to regard as a weak, simple-minded race, and the English settlers as a lot of rapacious, land absorbing native destroyers, from whose advent in New Zealand a wholesale demoralization, and rapid depopulation of native districts would result, and in a comparatively brief period the final extinction of the "Noble Savage" unless energetic measures were taken to avert it. In pursuance of this philanthropic object the party was organised, large sums subscribed, and there is no doubt considerable influence brought to bear upon the Home Government in the colonial appointments made, and they were represented in the colony by two salaried officers, styled the "Protectors of Aborigines."

It was the knowledge of the ruthless manner in which the American Indians had been dispossessed of their hunting grounds, and almost exterminated, that originated a movement that had for its object a laudable desire to avert such evils in the new field being opened for colonisation; but, like many other benevolent schemes, it was traded upon to a considerable extent, and had a natural tendency to run into extremes.

In the case of New Zealand, with a remarkably intelligent and warlike native race, that could neither be cowed nor overreached, and were quite capable of taking good care of themselves, much mischief resulted to the settlers, and also the natives, from the officious interference of irresponsible officers. But their mischievous antics in the colony culminated upon the burning of the town of Russell at Korororiki; and upon a full knowledge of the facts reaching the Home Government the colony was relieved of the incubus, by the governor and protectors being summarily swept away.

A Step Downward.

At the time of the founding of the Nelson Settlement there were very few natives located in the middle or what is now called the Southern Island; Rauparaha some years before having swept it from end to end, killing and burning all before him, and his savage ferocity not being satiated, he pressed an English ship into his service for the conveyance of his fighting party to the Chatham Islands, where a further war of extermination was carried on. There were consequently only some two or three hundred of the refugees living at the Motueka, Wakapuaka, and Queen Charlotte's Sound, and these were friendly and of great service in supplying needful produce to the settlers. They were remarkably shrewd at driving a bargain, had a very appreciative opinion of their commodities, and a critical knowledge of the value of the "utu," (money) and the goods taken in exchange. As they much preferred the Pakeha's blankets to their ordinary dog-skin, or flax mats, this was the only change of costume that had at that time been adopted, and they were to be seen in all the varied shades, and stages of wear, from the well worn and tattered specimen, to the snowy-white with resplendent border just out of the store. One storekeeper who did a large blanket trade with the Maoris and whose knowledge of their language was limited to the word kapai (good), was accustomed to express various degrees of excellence by a single, double, or treble repetition of the word kapai, to the great amusement of his swarthy customers, by which he acquired among them the sobriquet of "old Kapai."

Some of the native names of places were curiously transformed into familiar English words by the early settlers, for instance, Wakapuaka and Motueka, were Anglicised into Hokeepokee and Muddy-wake. Occasionally the natives when encamped in the township, either for their own amusement, or to please or terrify the on-lookers, would range themselves in a row, and sing or chant in a monotonous tone, what we supposed was a native song or poem—with a kind of chorus in which the arms were thrown alternately to the right and left, with a spasmodic twitching of the fingers, all acting in perfect time and concert; and with lolling tongues, and hideous contortion of the features, of which the carvings that adorn their houses and canoes were not very exaggerated fac-similes, at the same time producing a gutteral hissing sound from the chest, reminding one of the steam escaping from the cylinders of a locomotive engine when just starting.

CHAPTER III.

DISCARDED.

Mr. Tuckett, the chief surveyor, was with the party at the Wairau, but being a member of the "Society of Friends," and therefore not countenancing any steps of an aggressive character, had remained at a distance from the korero, and when he heard shots fired retreated at once to the boat at the mouth of the river, and was taken on board the brig. After the lamented death of his chief, he was for a time acting agent of the Company at Nelson, and during his brief tenure of the office, made fresh efforts to extend the small farm system that Captain Wakefield had initiated and encouraged.

As there were so few employers of labour

Discarded. 55

either engaged in farming or other works, there was a great redundancy of labour in the settlement; in this respect there was a failure of Edward Gibbon Wakefield's 'Theory of Colonization,' as capital had not been attracted in sufficient proportion to properly balance the labour element, or if attracted, it had been repelled by the pernicious system of allotment before referred to.

From whatever cause, the fact remained that there was a large number of men and families solely dependent upon the Company's employment; and when that should cease, with no tie to bind or attach them to the settlement.

Captain Wakefield therefore endeavoured to establish cottier farming, but with very limited success. About twenty families were settled in the Riwaka Valley, who being supplied with seed wheat and potatoes gratis, land upon easy terms, and employment in forming necessary roads in their neighbourhood, began vigorously to devote such little time as was not occupied in road making, to the cultivation of their land. A few provident families had been induced by the same encouragement to settle at the Waimea and Motueka; but the chief occupation at the latter place was sawing timber for the Nelson market, as there was a fine extent of bush unappropriated, that any one was free to enter to fell trees, and saw timber without let or hinderance. This gave occupation to a considerable number, as it was work at which novices soon acquire a fair proficiency.

As summer was approaching and some of our party being desirous of doing a little cultivating in the spare time of morning and evening, if land could be obtained in the neighbourhood of the work, the time on the road work being from 8 to 5, four of us resolved to apply to Mr. Tuckett for the lease of a 50 acre section with right of purchase, and the seed wheat and potatoes granted under such circumstances. E., not having anything to do at his own trade, was invited to join; he, the overseer, one of the road party, and myself, being the four applicants. The application was readily granted, and operations were immediately commenced as the season for sowing was fast slipping by. The section was admirably suited for our purpose, not only from its contiguity to our day work, but from its including a small wooded valley, which, being chiefly scrub and small trees, the larger trees being some distance apart, and only one here and there requiring to be felled, was easily cleared.

We soon had two acres cut down, burnt and cleared, and the wheat sown, chipping it into the rich loose bush mould with adzes, and we shortly had the satisfaction of witnessing its dark green verdure giving promise of a luxuriant crop.

As December was the season for potato planting, there was plenty of time to get a good patch cleared; we were very busy in the early mornings and evenings, often working by moonlight, and had made sad havoc with a beautiful stretch of bush that was ruthlessly laid low before our axes, when orders came for the summary removal of our road party to assist in cutting a large ditch through a swamp at the Waimea. This brought our agricultural operations to a sudden standstill, our only consolation under the circumstances being the knowledge that the wheat was growing, and that we had as much land cleared for potatoes as we were likely to procure sufficient seed to plant, as two or three months of summer sun would render the brushwood cut down so combustible, that when fired it would leave the ground in such a clear state, that no after labour would be required but planting the seed.

During the next two or three months the change was consummated to which I have already referred. No boat-building work offering, I continued at the road work, and as its distance from town necessitated an enforced absence all the week, my opportunities for counteracting a change that was gradually, but surely taking place, were necessarily limited.

For some time it was felt rather than perceived, and fearful of giving way to what might be only the promptings of jealousy, I fought against the vague suspicion, lest any action of mine should precipitate a change that I could not help feeling was impending.

Discarded.

And so matters progressed until it was no longer possible to mistake the altered feeling of my fiancée. There was a rude awakening from what had been a very pleasant, all absorbing day dream, a crushing blow to many fond anticipations, accompanied with a sensitive consciousness that could not help contrasting my, at that time, comparatively hopeless position and prospects, with the superior advantages enjoyed by my rival, which deprived me of all power of protest and resistance. I had many reasons for believing that she had also long struggled against a change, that circumstances had in a great measure rendered inevitable.

On arriving on Monday morning at the scene of our future work, I found several gangs of men concentrated upon one spot, which from the limited out-look afforded me, standing as I was knee deep in water in a dense mass of bulrushes, which reached far above my head, I judged to be near the centre of a large swamp; we had had to scramble for about a quarter of a mile through the rushes and slough to reach this position.

I could not help wondering how any number of men set down in the middle of a swamp like that, were going to solve the engineering difficulty of draining it without some outlet.

I afterwards learnt that another party of men were working towards us from seaward, and had completed from fifty to sixty chains of ditching, but in the meantime we were isolated, and working at great discomfort, and under serious disadvantages for the due progress of the work.

I also very soon discovered another innovation that was freely commented on by the men in no very complimentary terms, namely, the presence of a time-keeper whose duty we were informed it was to deduct an hour from each man's time who paused from work for a few minutes.

These and other vexatious changes, and our position in that part of the swamp, were for some reason that I never learnt attributed to the influence of a Frenchman named Vallie, who henceforth was to have complete control and superintendence of the men and works.

Discarded. 61

He was expected to visit the work in the swamp during the week, and there was some kind of understanding between a section of the men to be revenged upon him in some way.

About the middle of the week he made his appearance equipped in a pair of long boots and an eye-glass ; I don't mean in quite the style of the native chief who upon being requested by the missionary to set an example to the others attending church, by putting on some clothing next time, appeared in a pair of boots and a paper collar. As he neared the scene of operations, stepping nimbly from tussock to tussock, unfortunately for himself he first encountered the advanced guard of the party who had resolved to signalize the honour paid them by his visit.

The first symptom of insubordination was by one of the men coolly surveying him in true theatrical style through a piece of flax, twisted up in the form of an eye-glass, and as this marked attention was not fully appreciated, but on the contrary provoked some threatening language, a number of the men immediately began to display great activity in tying flax together to form a rope, on perceiving which and divining something threatening in their looks and actions, he commenced a hasty retreat, not pausing this time to step from tussock to tussock, but plunging recklessly through the slough and water, followed by about 30 or 40 of the men. On emerging from the bulrushes the party came out where the other men before referred to were ditching —here a long section of the ditch had been dammed in order to bottom another portion of it and was consequently full of water to the surface.

While walking alongside of this with a numerous and noisy retinue, he either slipped, in his trepidation, or was pushed in, and for a minute or so was floundering in a very inglorious manner in a seven-foot ditch of very dirty water.

He was quickly extricated, however, and after being tenderly tilted, to empty the water from his long boots, was permitted to quietly retire, with very dampened spirits from his moist reception.

A charge was laid against one man, and he was lodged in gaol, but it, the gaol, was of such a primitive character that his comrades found no difficulty in unceremoniously liberating him, and I do not remember any further proceedings being taken in the matter.

Mr. Vallic, after his involuntary bath, retired from the appointment, considering it impracticable to manage such an unruly lot of men, and the public works resumed their accustomed serenity. After working some time in the swamp, the party I was engaged with (for I may observe the men were divided into gangs of about twenty, with an overlooker to each gang) was drafted to another part of the Waimea, where the work being dry, it was much pleasanter, and shortly after this change came another still more agreeable.

Mr. Fox had succeeded Mr. Tuckett as the Company's agent, and in order to facilitate the cultivation of land by the men employed on the Company's works, initiated a system of piece work on the roads, but limiting the quantity to be executed each week to what was considered an average week's work by day work, paying the same wages, but allowing the men to do the required quantity in as short a time as possible, by which arrangement they would have more time to devote to their cultivations, and the Company's work would not suffer.

This was a very politic and wise arrangement, as there was not only a marked increase in the amount of work executed each week, but there is no doubt it materially assisted to permanently settle many families of the working class in the settlement, who would otherwise have left on the suspension of the Company's expenditure, which took place about nine months later.

By this time I had become so well accustomed to the work, that on the introduction of piece work, I could execute my portion as well and expeditiously as any of them, namely, in two and a half or three days, though it took some four and five days to complete the required quantity.

The allowance was twenty four cubic yards of ditching, including the pitching the earth, and forming the road a chain wide, but leaving

Discarded. 65

a clear space of seven feet between the made road and ditch on either side; this involved pitching the earth a long distance, and I remember there used to be frequent disputes between parties working on opposite sides of the road about filling up the centre, some not throwing the earth far enough. The price was 9d. per cube yard, or 18s. for the week's work as before. It was considered such good pay at the time, that for a few weeks, until prevented by fresh regulations, many left their ordinary occupations to engage in it.

Blacksmiths left their anvils, town-carriers their teams, and in a few instances shopkeepers their counters, and returned to their usual employment for the remainder of the week.

And yet it required downright hard physical exertion, and longer hours each day, so to shorten the time in which to complete the allotted task, as would then only make it equal to the present ordinary pay of a day labourer, namely, 8s. per day.

When the agent discovered that many were taking advantage of the arrangement without

F

having taken land, or intended taking any, it was ordered that all such should no longer be allowed a share in the employment. A clerk was deputed to visit all engaged on the works, and take down the quantity of land owned, and in cultivation; or the quantity and situation of any land a workman was willing to occupy and cultivate, a negative answer to all of which being a summary dismissal from the work. One man, owner of a cart and pair of bullocks, and whose ordinary employment was as town-carrier, but who had found it advantageous to do the quantum of piece work so long as the condition of taking and cultivating land was not insisted on, was waited upon by the collector, and in answer to the query of how much land he was prepared to take, said, with ironical gravity, pointing to a large hill near his dwelling, at the entrance of Brook Street Valley, "put ma doon th' whole o' th' Sugar-loaf Mountain."

While I was thus occupied December was near at hand, and it became necessary to see about the potato planting; some time before this E. had crossed the bay to build a boat for some young men residing there, and had not yet returned.

Upon visiting the scene of our former labours and making inquiries, I found that one of the original quartette, the overseer, taking advantage of our absence (for the remaining partner had disappeared I knew not whither), had sold his and our interest in the cultivations without our knowledge or consent, so all our labour was lost and we could get no redress.

Up to this period I had continued as one of the family at E.'s, still regarding their house as my home, notwithstanding my altered relations to one of its members; but this arrangement I felt could not be continued much longer. To be received with coldness and indifference by one upon whom I once had centred all my hopes of happiness, was painful and depressing to a degree, but to be the voluntary witness of endearments lavished upon another, I felt was subjecting myself to an unnecessary trial of my fortitude that it would be wise to avoid.

E. had now found employment at his own

business, so I thought it a fair opportunity to retire, and provide a home for myself elsewhere.

Upon his return from the Riwaka, and finding that I had left the house, and made a beginning upon my own account, he strongly advised me to go to the Riwaka to settle; telling me it was a very pretty valley, with plenty of good land, and nearly all the residents well known to me, they having been fellow-passengers in the 'Indus,' and Company's work to be had on the same terms as on the Nelson side.

I thought the best course to pursue was to follow his advice, and accordingly removed to the Riwaka, arriving there on new year's day, 1844. So one eventful year had nearly passed away since that memorable morning in February, when, the prospect taking its tone from the gladsome mind of the observers, all appeared so fair, so bright, and charming.

CHAPTER IV.

ARCADIAN.

As companionship was preferable to lonely brooding, I joined labour with a young man with whom I had been on friendly terms on board ship, and in the endeavour to improve the present, as far as possible to ignore the past.

It was midsummer, and the weather extremely hot, and as the road work lay at some distance, it was our custom to begin it very early in the morning, carrying a kettle and the materials for breakfast with us, and having that meal on the spot after two or three hour's work—and completing the portion we allotted for the day, in time to return to a one o'clock dinner.

The remainder of the day was generally devoted to work on the land, but at this time I was busily employed in the erection of a house of a temporary kind; but from an accident to a more ambitious structure, also in hand at this time, it had to do duty for nearly eighteen months.

The temporary one was of the V hut fashion, except that it was built upon piles six feet high instead of on the ground. Upon these posts a floor was laid and roofed, and therefore it resembled a small house with the walls unenclosed, and being situate in a thick bush, and well sheltered, this was of no great consequence. Some cross pieces nailed to the posts, and a small opening in the floor, gave access to a warm and snug sleeping apartment during the winter, but when summer came I found I had constructed an admirable mosquito trap, or else it was so highly appreciated that they made it their head-quarters, for when I ascended my rustic stairs at night, and entered the sleeping-room, it was like taking possession of a bee-hive. Day by day as summer advanced, fresh cohorts arrived to swell their ranks, and I was upon the point of leaving them in undisputed possession of the place, when a happy expedient of circumventing them suggested itself. It was neither more nor less than ensconcing my head in the pillow-case, and though an intrusive proboscis occasionally penetrated even that, upon the whole I was victorious, as their incessant buzzing did not prevent my sleeping.

At a short distance in the open land, and upon a gentle rise, I began the erection of a clay house with walls one foot thick—the earth being firmly rammed between two stout mould boards, which were so arranged that they could be shifted as the work progressed. I was engaged upon this work at odd times for about three months, with occasional assistance for which I had to work in return, and had completed the walls, and laid the wall plates ready for receiving the roof, when one of those autumn storms of wind and rain, that frequently usher in the winter season, came on with unusual violence. The result was that the walls exposed to the driving rain, softened and fell one after the other, and being too late in the season to begin another of the same kind, I had to be contented with the hut first built.

It was a serious disappointment to find that I had been misinformed as to the rate of pay and the diminution to which I should have to submit in the future. Whereas on the Nelson side of the bay I received 18s. for twenty-four yards of ditching, at the Riwaka 10s. only was paid weekly for the same amount of work. I found upon seeking for an explanation of this disparity, and the inadequate wages for so much work, that I suffered in my individual position as a single man, unconnected with any family, from the adoption of a system that was intended to operate favourably for heads of families, that included among its members several sons who were allowed to take the piece work the same as their fathers, but at a lower rate of pay, namely, 10s. per week, while heads of families received the full amount.

I felt obliged to accept the position, and submit to what I could not help thinking was an injustice, as the only alternative was to

Arcadian. 73

return to Nelson, to which I had a very great objection.

The cost of living was also increased by the conveyance of all provisions across the bay, and with flour at 22s. 6d. per 100 lbs., it reduced my wages to about the same rate, if not below the level of the English agricultural labourer, which I had always heard cited as only a short remove from starvation point; but little as it was, I was grieved to lose it a few months later, when the work's expenditure entirely ceased.

I here wish to tender my humble tribute to the kindly interest taken by Mr. Fox, the Company's agent, in anything and everything likely to assist or improve the position of all the Company's employés who showed an earnest desire of rendering themselves independent of such assistance, by cultivating their land. He suggested to some of the heads of families in the valley the great advantage to be derived from the establishment of a store, by which we should be in a great measure independent of the precarious visits of the boat, and also, by purchasing wholesale, reduce the prices of articles of general consumption to some extent. He at the same time offering to advance an amount equal to two months' wages, as a capital to stock it, and for it to be managed upon the co-operative principle.

This generous offer was thankfully and gladly accepted; by combined labour a suitable weather-boarded building was quickly erected, and stocked with the staple articles of consumption. One who was considered the most suitable for the office was elected manager, and his allotment of road-work being equally distributed among us, so that he could continue to draw his usual wages, no cost for management was incurred, and by purchasing wholesale, and Mr. Fox having kindly arranged that the supplies should be sent across the bay in the Company's boat free of charge, an important saving to the consumer was the net result.

The store was of great benefit to all concerned, as besides lessening the cost of living, the vicissitudes to which the supplies had often been subjected were in a great measure avoided, as very often the boat could not cross the bay when provisions were much needed, which necessarily caused considerable inconvenience to families whose means did not enable them to provide against contingencies of this nature.

Even after the establishment of the store there were occasions when the stock of flour, etc., became exhausted before fresh supplies could be received, but these were of much rarer occurrence than formerly. Upon one occasion of this kind, after a period of enforced fasting, when fresh supplies had come to hand, and every one was supplied with their usual quantity,—a member of a large family presented himself at the store for a second 200 lb. bag of flour, very shortly after having received the first. Bumble was not more surprised at the temerity of little Oliver asking for more, than was the storekeeper, and he could not help inquiring what had become of the first bag, when the lad replied, "Woy! we set up o' nights eating it, s'long as it lasted."

The starting of this store was a happy illustration of the amount of good that may be dispensed among a great number, by a large employer of labour having a generous forethought for what interests and concerns his employés, without necessarily entailing pecuniary considerations or assistance, and its frequent concomitants, loss of self-respect and independence.

I have previously referred to the aptitude displayed by the early settlers for all kinds of bush work, such as felling trees and sawing timber, if located near a bush, and as there were several fine patches of bush in the valley at the time of its being first settled, no time was lost in turning the timber to account for house building, etc. One middle-aged man, head of a large family, who had probably never seen a pit saw before he came to New Zealand, had with his sons' assistance dug saw pits, and while his two eldest sons were sawing at one pit, as if they had been accustomed to the work for a number of years, the old man might have been seen at another pit, sawing away on the top of a huge log, with a younger son, aged about 14, in the pit, actually standing upon a stool to enable him to swing the long pit saw the necessary length of stroke.

I heard of one amateur pitman whose ignorance nearly resulted in a serious accident; the log while being sawn rests upon movable cross-pieces called transoms, and it is the duty of the man in the pit to give the signal to halt when it is necessary to shift the transom.

Upon the occasion referred to, the log being large, the top-sawyer could not tell exactly when to stop, but was momentarily expecting the signal to do so from his mate in the pit; at last he inquired if he had not reached the transom. "Yes!" replied his mate, "and nearly through it;" it may be guessed it did not take that man many seconds to descend from his perilous position, and thrust a spare transom beneath the log.

The management of the store continued in the same hands, and gave general satisfaction, until the end of the second quarter, when the balance-sheet submitted by the storekeeper showed a deficiency of about twenty pounds, for which he could not account; he asked my help to go with him through all the items, and check the extensions, etc., which I did, and still the mysterious deficiency remained unexplained. A public meeting was called, and some present in very plain terms impugned the honesty of the storekeeper.

A resolution was passed removing him from his office, and demanding the surrender of the books; but smarting under the undeserved suspicions, and conscious that some error remained undetected, which the resigning of the books at that time would deprive him of all chance of discovering, he resolutely refused to give them up at that stage of the proceedings, unless to some one they might appoint competent to examine them. Another resolution was passed appointing a deputation to go to Nelson, and inform Mr. Fox of the whole of the particulars, and of the storekeeper's refusal to surrender the books.

I and another were the only dissentients, feeling sure that some satisfactory explanation would be found before long, and we sympathised with him for the hasty and unjust aspersions cast upon him.

Late that evening he informed me it was the intention of the deputation to start next day by boat for Nelson, and that he had determined to start very early in the morning to walk to Nelson, carrying the books, and if possible to deliver them to Mr. Fox, before the arrival of the deputation, which he thought was quite feasible, as the boat being at the end of the road, it could not get away before noon at high water; so the deputation would not arrive in time to wait upon Mr. Fox before the following day.

As it was a long distance (about 40 miles) through only partially explored country, and several rivers to be crossed on the route, he asked me to accompany him on the journey, which I readily agreed to do.

It was July or mid-winter, and a journey overland at that time of the year, with the rivers above their ordinary level, and their extent and the nature of the country to be traversed then unknown, was no light undertaking, and would have been positively hazardous for one alone. About eighteen months before this, four of the residents made the journey in company in the summer time, and were four days doing it, and suffered great hardships from exposure and want of food. We felt quite confident of reaching Nelson the same evening. We started about 4 A.M., and as we walked over the crisp grass, the white hoar frost glistened in the bright moonlight; as the first half-hour's walk would bring us to the Motueka River, and an immediate plunge into that not being a very cheering process in the early morning, we resolved to make a detour to a deserted Maori pah, near the mouth of the river, where we knew there was an unfinished canoe on the stocks. It had been probably many years in the state we found it, its sides were fairly shaped, but in other respects it was little more than a log of wood, and we had serious misgivings about its answering our purpose; however, we resolved to try it. After an hour's great exertions, with the help of rollers and levers we at last succeeded in getting the ungainly thing into the water, when upon stepping into it, to our dismay and disappointment, it revolved like a barrel, and as this part of the river was wide

Arcadian. 81

and deep, and the current strong, we were obliged to abandon it, and reluctantly retrace our steps up the river and take the first apparently eligible ford; as having lost so much valuable time, we did not care to go as far as the known ford, at which the river was usually crossed. Fortunately my companion was a few inches taller than myself, and by holding his hand, the passage was safely effected, but at one part, where the water reached my waistcoat pockets, I felt so extremely buoyant in the swift current that I durst not raise my feet, but was obliged to shuffle along or I should certainly have lost my footing, which would have probably resulted in the discomfiture of us both. After taking off our wet clothes, and effecting a mutual wringing out of the surplus water, we resumed our damp attire and the journey. We had travelled about eight miles when another river crossed our route, but this was small compared to the previous one, and the only inconvenience was a fresh wetting, just as we were getting comfortably dry.

Shortly after crossing this river, and coming

G

upon a thick bush, we were beguiled into taking a surveyor's line that appeared to lead through it, instead of ascending a range of hills that here ran almost parallel with the bush, and by which we should have saved a great deal of time, and avoided much fatigue and difficulty. The line we had chosen was the surveyor's base line through the Moutere valley bush, and base enough we found it; the bush was so dense and thick, with supple-jack and undergrowth of all kinds, that we could not deviate to either side of the line, and a winding river running through it, that was no sooner crossed with difficulty in one place, than it presented itself unexpectedly again in another short distance, and this occurred so often that we became quite bewildered as to which side of it was our proper one. This river was not more than five or six yards in width, but deep and sluggish, with a great quantity of timber in it, and we effected one crossing by climbing a tree that had been splintered off about fifteen feet from the ground, and descending the broken part, which remained attached to the trunk and extended across the river at an angle of about 45 degrees.

Appearances began to indicate that we were nearing the boundary of the bush. We were just congratulating ourselves upon having overcome all the difficulties of this route, when we found ourselves hemmed in by a bull-rush swamp.

It deepened as we advanced, so we deemed it prudent to climb a tree to reconnoitre. We found it to be of considerable extent, the centre part being clear of rushes indicated deep water, and as unfortunately neither of us could swim, we were obliged to wend our weary way back again for some distance to where we had noticed a steep hill abutting close to the bush, to ascend the hill, and descend again into the valley beyond the limits of the swamp.

In this valley, or rather crescent-shaped block of open land, almost surrounded by bush, a range of hills forming the chord of the arc, a number of Germans had settled. On the side of the hill as we descended, we passed close by the frame of a building apparently intended for a church, but it continued in the same unfinished state for several years, when it was either taken or blown down.

The Germans had arrived the previous year in the St. Pauli; some of them were wine-growers, and they entertained the delusion that in this sheltered spot vines could be cultivated with the same success as in the South of France; but a very brief experience sufficed to correct this mistake, and after a few years, only a few still lingered in the neighbourhood, doing a little farming, but now there is quite a thriving village a short distance from the spot, with its school and church, and road-side inn, kept by one of the original Germans, and where the Royal Mail Coach stops an hour for passengers and horses to refresh, it being about midway between Nelson and Motueka.

After crossing this open land, and passing through another portion of the same bush, but skirting the hills, evening began to close in, so we thought it advisable to seek temporary rest and shelter in one of the huts near at hand, until the moon rose, when we proposed continuing our journey as the remainder of the route appeared to be open country.

We had only provided sufficient food for one meal when starting, supposing Nelson would be reached the same evening, and as this had been disposed of about mid-day, we were quite prepared to do justice to a good supper, had it been in the power of our entertainer to have provided such a luxury. Unfortunately he had nothing but a few cobs of Indian corn and some very small potatoes on the premises; we accepted a place by the fire and a cob of corn, and amused ourselves during the evening in munching the very hard fare.

The hut was built of young birch-trees about six inches in diameter; it might be called a log-house, with the logs ranged vertically, and being let into the ground about a couple of feet, gave stability to the structure. The space inside was about 8 feet by 12, with a thatched roof; and at one end a fireplace formed with logs the same as the sides, but not so high, and lined inside with clay.

Its usual occupants appeared to be the one we first accosted, a man about 40, and four strapping youths, his sons I supposed, and they were employed forming a road through a portion of the bush. In the course of the evening they, one by one, stretched themselves upon the hard clay floor, and soon gave oracular demonstration of the truth of Shakespeare's words, that

"Labour can snore upon the rock."

I am not quite sure of the correctness of the quotation, but I do know the nasal chorus effectually relieved us from all apprehension of ourselves falling asleep, which from very weariness we might otherwise have done, and thereby missed the opportunity of resuming our journey so soon as the moon should light our route, which would not be until two or three o'clock in the morning, and for whose coming light we frequently cast anxious glances up the chimney, or, perhaps more correctly, out of the fireplace.

I had been rather surprised at the absence of all sleeping arrangements, as in the roughest colonial wharé there is generally one or more places fitted up called bunks, and supposed they had another building to which they retired to sleep.

This primitive style of lying down in their clothes was evidently not due to the presence of strangers, as there being no vestige of blankets or bedding, favoured the supposition that this was their ordinary method of taking their night's rest.

At last we could distinguish the moon's silver light above the glare of the roaring fire we had been instructed to keep up, but legs and arms were so inextricably mingled on the floor that exit by the door seemed next to impossible without treading upon, or disturbing one or more of the sleepers; so finding escape by the chimney practicable, we were soon once more on the road, and as there was a well-defined track and open country over the range of hills to the Waimea plain there was no fear of our mistaking the road. Just at daylight we were descending the hills into the Waimea Plain, the winding course of the Wairoa River, distant about two miles, clearly defined by a line of white mist, its wintry veil, which was being slowly stirred into fantastic shapes by the gentle morning breeze. We were prosaic enough to think that a boat or a bridge, by which we should have been saved the necessity of wading through the river, would have been a more charming sight than any amount of picturesque scenery that cold morning.

I glanced at my companion and noticed that his whiskers were white with rime; I instinctively felt my own, and found them quite crisp with the frost. I suggested the advantage of taking off our socks before wading the river, as it would be so comfortable to have them dry to walk in afterwards, but on attempting to unlace my boots for this purpose, I found my fingers quite powerless from the cold, although I was not sensible of any sensation of coldness in them; my companion was in the same predicament, so we were obliged to let them remain.

We reached Kite's hostelry at Richmond about nine o'clock, and as we had not broken our fast since noon of the preceding day, and had undergone a considerable amount of wear

Arcadian. 89

and tear in the interval, we were tolerably hungry, and watched with some interest and impatience the preparations for breakfast.

Mrs. K. with true womanly instinct divined our condition and thoughts, and asked us if we would like a snack to begin with, while the chops were frying, to which we cordially assented, and a pork pie, made in an oval pie-dish, the long diameter of which was about ten inches, was set before us, the complete consumption of which was so nicely timed that the last particle of it had just disappeared as the chops were served up, upon which we then proceeded to make an ordinary breakfast. We arrived in Nelson about mid-day, and found the Riwaka boat had only preceded us by an hour; the deputation had waited upon Mr. Fox and reported the state of affairs and the refusal of the storekeeper to give up the books, when that much-abused individual appeared on the scene, to the great astonishment of the deputation, as our departure had been kept secret. He delivered up the books to Mr. Fox, with the request that he would be pleased to allow the Company's accountant to examine them, which he very graciously agreed should be done.

The error, or rather omission, was accidentally discovered in the course of the day, by the Company's storekeeper casually remarking that a certain Nelson merchant from whom the supplies had been chiefly received, had not only charged his ordinary prices for stores, but added 5 per cent. commission for purchasing the goods, at the same time supplying them chiefly from his own store. This was the missing link, credit had not been taken in the balance-sheet for this commission, which had been paid, and for the period under review exactly covered the amount deficient.

Explanations immediately followed, Mr. Fox was perfectly satisfied, but I cannot say the deputation were, although obliged to accept the agent's decision in the matter. It appeared to have been a foregone conclusion in their minds, that all was not as it should be, and having made grave charges, they could not conceive of their being susceptible of such a simple solution; and from their report resulting in a confirmation of the previous dismissal of the storekeeper, it was evident they continued under their former impression, and they believed that Mr. Fox, with characteristic generosity, had intervened to screen him.

I was so annoyed with this result that I withdrew my name from the list of members, thereby forfeiting my share and interest in the concern.

The storekeeper above referred to is now, and has been many years, an accountant in one of the departments of the General Government. The following year, having to make the same journey just described, having visited Nelson, and missed my passage by the return boat, I did it easily in twelve hours, but took the precaution of keeping on the range of hills between the Waimea and Moutere plains, carefully avoiding the wooded valley; but some years later, when a coach-road was opened through it, thereby lessening the distance some few miles, I have frequently walked it in less time and with less fatigue.

Two months after the store affair, or the beginning of September, 1844, news arrived of the suspension of the New Zealand Company's operations, and there was a consequent sudden stoppage of the road expenditure.

I was very ill prepared for this; small as the weekly pittance had been for the amount of work done for it, it was only with the utmost economy I had made it suffice for ordinary wants, and so far I had only succeeded in saving a shilling or two each month, which was immediately invested in seed potatoes. I considered myself fortunate in having on hand five large kits, about four cwt., at this time.

I heard there was in the store at the time of the works being stopped, about £150 worth of stock; while there was a debt due to the Company's agent of about £90. When Mr. Fox was communicated with in reference to discharging this debt, he generously waived it in favour of the residents in the valley.

I wish I could report that the Committee of Management were equally generous, for we were all sufferers in common from the stoppage of the works. Although I had voluntarily forfeited my share of the profits, which I had assisted to make, and my interest in the building I had assisted to erect, the ex-storekeeper and myself were also excluded from all participation in the generous gift of the agent, in the general division that took place of the store and its contents.

The piece of land I was preparing for cropping with potatoes was bush-land that had been cleared and planted by the Maories; it had been a fine piece of bush which Mr. Tuckett had granted them permission to clear and plant for one crop only, it being one of the Company's fifty-acre sections.

The part referred to was covered with fallen trees, and partly burnt logs, and had been planted in their usual style, namely, by simply forcing a pointed stick into the soil at an acute angle, loosening the ground slightly by a downward leverage, and inserting the seed. By cross-cutting the logs and rolling them together in heaps, and systematically grubbing the whole of the service, and taking out all but the largest roots, I was sanguine of obtaining a good crop of potatoes the ensuing season, and in this I was not disappointed. I had previously cleared and sown a half acre of wheat on part of the same land, and its luxuriant growth promised a satisfactory solution of the food supply question after harvest, but there were four months intervening that I had to tide over as I best could.

My immediate wants were fortunately provided by my daily work; it had been impossible for the Maories to extract all the potatoes from among the matted roots, and in going over every inch of the ground with an adze, I obtained each day sufficient for its consumption.

I was thus occupied the whole of September and October, and judging that there was enough land prepared for the quantity of seed I possessed, and finding that an almost exclusive potato diet was not very sustaining if continued too long, even when stimulated occasionally by a little wild pork, I resolved to take an opportunity that presented itself of earning a bag of flour, as there was a month or six weeks to spare before potato planting commenced.

Arcadian.

A gentleman, who owned a large portion of the upper part of the valley, was desirous of having a wooded knoll cleared of the bush, and the land grubbed and prepared for laying down in English grass, as it had a fine commanding position for a residence.

CHAPTER V.

HARD LINES.

At the time I came upon the scene the large timber had been felled, cross-cut and cleared off, and the work requiring to be done was the same I had been for some time engaged at, namely, all the roots to be grubbed up, large and small; large ones to be cut close to the stumps, closer indeed than I had cut my own, which involved an immense amount of chopping and levering, as the roots of New Zealand trees are mostly on or near the surface, are very large near the stumps, and radiate all round for a great distance, especially the white pine, and this bush was chiefly of this kind of timber. The price offered for this work was $7\frac{1}{2}d.$ the rod of $5\frac{1}{2}$ yds. square, and I knew by experience that I should

Hard Lines.

have to work very hard, and very late to average four rods a day;—but I had been without flour so long that I agreed to do as many rods as would outset a 200 lb. bag, which at the price of flour at that time occupied me three weeks.

I was now virtually independent in my own estimation; before the flour would be exhausted, my wheat crop would be harvested, and though not more than sufficient for my wants and for seed, there would be several tons of potatoes to sell, which would provide everything else required.

As my left hand lies upon the paper while writing this, each finger bears evidence of that and subsequent harvests, from the awkwardness of the amateur reaper in the use of the sickle.

This was the only occasion upon which I worked for wages after the stoppage of the road-work, during the remainder of my residence in the valley, excepting the assisting a party temporarily who had taken a contract to procure a quantity of spars for a Nelson merchant.

I cannot help contrasting the greatly improved position of the ordinary labourer of the present time, as regards the rate of wages, prices of provisions, and general articles of consumption, and the command of the comforts and conveniences of an advanced state of Society, with the period of which I have been writing.

At the present time flower is about 28*s*. the 200 lb. bag, and an ordinary day-labourer is paid 8*s*. per day of eight hours, consequently he can earn in 3½ days a sack of flour, for which I wrought as many weeks, and had to work very hard, and for longer hours each day.

Soon after planting the potatoes I applied myself vigorously to the erection of a house, similar to the one that had come to grief the previous year, and with assistance, which had to be repaid in labour, it was finished before harvest.

After harvest I found it very useful for storing the crop, as by laying scantling across from wall to wall, the upper part of the house just contained it, leaving plenty of space in the lower part, the wheat forming a ceiling to the apartment. As the height was only about seven feet, which would not allow of the use of a flail for thrashing, I procured a round block of wood three feet in length and eighteen inches in diameter, and upon this I thrashed out the wheat as required, by taking as much of a sheaf as could be held by both hands and slashing it across the block until the corn was all knocked out of the ears, a slow process, but fairly effective, as from being stored in the house, where there was generally a good fire burning (as fire-wood was very plentiful), the corn was very dry and easily shed.

At this time a young man, who occupied the section adjoining mine, and the person I referred to as having assisted at the interment at the Wairau, proposed to join me, and work our land together. To this I assented, so he took up his abode with me, and we made common property of our few possessions. Ours was a very amicable partnership, and though only lasting twelve months, was only terminated by our entering into another partnership of a more ambitious character, to which I shall refer in due course. We shared some hard times very cheerfully together, and from being so happily suited to each other I suppose, we never had a single disagreement, or an angry word pass between us while we lived together, or since for that matter, for though we have been widely sundered, living in different provinces, we have often had business transactions together to our mutual satisfaction and advantage. As his was chiefly fern land, requiring more labour to cultivate it and yielding less return for the labour, and the cleared part of my bush land being of but small extent, we resolved to squat upon, and prepare for the next season's wheat crop, a piece of unoccupied land near the river, that had formerly been a Maori clearing.

The soil we knew to be very good, and being of a light loamy nature, was very easy to dig, an important consideration when from the absence of oxen, horses, and ploughs, all our cultivating had to be done with the spade.

The land in question was covered with a

Hard Lines.

thick verdure of wild weeds, the creeping chick-weed predominating, a sure indication of the fertility of the soil, and it required deep and careful digging to bury the thick surface growth. We used to dig ten rods a day each; in fact we made it a set task to accomplish this much, by pacing out the distance to be dug each day. I remember our plan was to divide the day's work into certain stages, putting in a stick at a certain distance, and digging to it before stopping for a rest and smoke; then pacing and marking the next point to be reached (generally rather more than half the day's task) when we would stop for dinner, and so on for the entire day's work. In this way four acres were dug in good seed time, and sown with wheat, we harrowing it, by drawing a large bundle of brushwood to and fro over the surface until the grain was well buried, a very toilsome operation from our having to walk so continuously over the loose soil. It was, indeed, farming under difficulties in the absence of nearly all the usual appliances, and was limited entirely to manual labour. There have not been wanting theorists who have advocated the superiority of spade husbandry, but my practical experience would incline me to prefer guiding a plough to using a spade for this purpose, even though the yield might be less prolific.

I remember looking round, and observing what a small proportion the result of three or four days' hard work bore to the entire plot, and feeling almost disheartened at the prospect, but as day by day added to the one, and diminished the other, the work seemed to grow less monotonous, and proceeded more lightly and cheerfully, and it was with a feeling of gleeful satisfaction that the last corner was rounded in.

After this, it seemed a light sort of pastime to dig an acre for barley, our spades were like burnished steel with the constant friction, and were very carefully housed at night, to preserve them in good working order, an old file being in constant requisition during the day to keep a good edge on them.

It was our custom to thrash upon wet days only, when no out-door work could be done, and it often happened from a continuance of fine

Hard Lines. 103

weather, that our supply of flower would become exhausted ; but we would not waste fine weather for such a trifling matter, and contented ourselves with potatoes only until the next wet day.

Upon awaking in the morning, and hearing the rain falling, we would rise early, get out the block, thrash out, and winnow about a bushel of wheat (we knew to a nicety how many sheaves to thrash), and carry it down the valley to the house of the owner of a hand flower-mill, the only one in the place, for the use of which 1s. per bushel was charged, with the privilege of grinding the wheat ourselves ; the thrashing, winnowing, and grinding occupying the entire day. This quantity we could make last a month, by making bread of about equal quantities of flower and potatoes, and this was the formula : as much flower added to mashed potatoes as would make a stiff dough, no water being used, and the loaf baked by placing it on the hot hearth, and covering it with hot wood, ashes, and embers. It would come out quite clean and light, and was simply delicious, the only fault being there was never enough of it, as we could only afford a small piece each as a relish with our tea, having first made our principal meal off potatoes. Our tea, I should remark, was made from the dried leaves of a native shrub, of a very spicy flavour, and known as the kawakawa, too pungent if used fresh and green, so we always had a branch hanging near the fireplace, from which a few leaves were stripped as required, and put in the tea-pot, and an infusion made as with ordinary tea, and milk being added (for at this time there were two cows in the valley), it made a very agreeable beverage; sugar we had none, but it did not seem to require it. I am convinced it must have possessed very refreshing and sustaining properties, otherwise I am sure with our spare diet, and continuous hard work, we could not have maintained such robust health and vigorous strength.

During the wheat grinding, I, upon one occasion, beguiled its tediousness for my partner and self, by reading aloud the first volume of Red Gauntlet, holding the book with one hand and turning the mill with the other, while my companion performed the "dem'd horrid grind," as Mantalini would have called it, at the other handle, deriving compensation in the interest of the story for any extra labour imposed.

While the digging of the four-acre field was in progress, we were favoured with an unusually long spell of fine weather, consequently had been without flour for some time, and as usual when out of flour, we had dispensed with the tea, not caring for it unless there was a piece of bread or damper to accompany it.

One morning at this time, when we had been without meat or flour for about a fortnight, I proposed roasting the potatoes for breakfast for a change, for I was beginning to feel dainty. Somehow I was not in my usual trim that morning at work, and at last I was obliged to lean upon my spade and was very sick. I felt too weak and ill to continue the work, and said as much to my companion. He replied that he also felt quite out of sorts. I then proposed our returning home and killing the pig in the sty, which was intended to have been kept for a future occasion; to this he cheerfully assented, and at noon that day, after having made a good square meal as a Yankee would say, we felt quite ourselves again.

As neither of us felt inclined to return to the digging, I resolved to signalize the sacrifice of the pig by a little experimental cookery, that I had been revolving in my mind for some time, and had only been waiting for an opportunity to put in practice; it was the manufacture of a haggis, and now the long-wished-for chance presented itself.

It would be absurd to take credit for any originality in relation to a subject, or dish, long ago immortalized by Robert Burns.

A few months previously, I had tasted this national dainty at a neighbour's house, and relishing it very much, was curious to inquire the secret of its composition, and now with the materials at hand I felt quite competent to undertake its preparation for our joint benefit, and imparted my intention to my companion, who, being a Scotchman, was pleased, perhaps a little flattered, at my enthusiasm in what might be considered his country's cause, and watched with absorbing interest my culinary preparations.

In the course of the momentous proceedings I discovered one important element wanting, namely, oatmeal; what was to be done? Were we to be defeated for such a trifle? No, indeed! We had some bran in the house. Why should not that do as well? Accordingly, as much bran was added as gave the requisite cohesion to the ingredients, and now the matchless deed was achieved, and the haggis all ready for cooking; but this was deferred until the evening, when we should be sufficiently at leisure to give our entire minds to its attention and contemplation.

Accordingly, in the evening, we were sitting on either side of the fireplace, smoking our pipes and pleasantly chatting, while the music of the bubbling pot formed a grateful accompaniment, when we were nearly startled off our seats by a loud explosion in the pot. The melancholy fact was soon disclosed; the haggis had burst; sufficient allowance had not been made for the swelling of the bran, and a large pot of soup was the result.

This was a serious disappointment, but it was not to be borne that we should lose our supper by a mishap of this kind, so we regaled ourselves with a large basin of the soup each, and finished the remainder for breakfast next morning.

CHAPTER VI.

A FRESH START.

FAINT echoes of the doings in the North Island occasionally reached even this remote spot, though from the infrequent communication with the seat of Government, the latest news from Auckland was generally received in Nelson *viâ* Sydney.

During the year 1845, a chronic state of disturbance with the natives existed in the neighbourhood of Auckland, which was generally attributed to the mistaken policy of the governor. Conciliation had been carried to the verge of servility, and its natural and foretold result was, to make the natives more obstructive, arrogant, and turbulent; every concession being by them attributed to fear.

Johnnie Heki amused himself by cutting down the flag-staff each time it was raised; three times he performed this operation, but the fourth one he carried bodily away, saying with grim humour that the tree was his, he and his ancestors having been born under it; but there was little doubt his ire was kindled chiefly on the score of its being the emblem of sovereignty, and as such he appeared determined not to allow the flag to be flaunting defiance before him. Upon this latest reason for his opposition to the flag-staff being reported to the governor, he ordered the purchase of the mizen mast of a Chilian man-of-war for the purpose of a flag-staff, in order, it may be supposed, to be quite satisfied that no natives of New Zealand had been born under it. This temporising and truckling policy disgusted the settlers, and had the effect of leading the natives to despise all governmental authority, and the flag episode was soon followed by the sacking and burning of the town of Russell, the settlers gladly escaping with their lives, but with the loss of all their possessions.

A Fresh Start.

Governor Fitzroy was as unsuccessful in his government of the settlers as of the natives; the colonial finances were in a frightfully disorganised state; all the customs duties had been abolished, and the projected income tax that was to have provided the necessary funds for carrying on the government was found impossible to levy or collect, for the simple reason that, at that early date, no one was suspected of having any. Next a poll tax was proposed; and here at least there was the tangible fact of a man's existence and presence in the colony for a starting-point, but the difficulty of getting beyond that I suppose was found so great, that it also was abandoned and the old duties were re-imposed.

For the exigencies of the public service £15,000 worth of debentures were issued in sums of from 5s. to £50, and a deluge of 5s. "shin plasters" was the immediate result. They were held in such small esteem by the settlers, that their backs were made the vehicle for circulating remarks, the reverse of complimentary to the government and officials. Occasionally private individuals achieved unexpected notoriety by the same medium. I remember seeing one that bore the well-known phrase, of an equally well-known Wellington settler, that might be considered more forcible than polite,—it was, " I vill smash you like von bug."

A monster petition was prepared and signed by nearly all the Wellington and Nelson settlers, setting forth the grievances under which the colony was labouring; this was sent home for presentation to the Imperial Parliament.

Whether it had the desired effect, or the acts and policy of the governor became too patent and obnoxious to the Home Government, I know not, but early in October, 1845, intelligence reached Nelson that Governor Fitzroy was to be relieved of the government of New Zealand, and from the experience of storms political he afterwards directed his attention to the law of storms elemental, and achieved a fame in connection with the latter by which he is alone known to the present generation. I supposed his lieutenants, the

A Fresh Start. 113

two Clarks, the "Protectors of Aboriginees," fell with their chief, or were rendered innocuous, for very little was heard of them afterwards.

The news of the recall was received with great demonstrations of rejoicing in Nelson. A public open-air dinner was organised, and subscribed for in cash and kind by every one in the settlement.

It came off on a large open space near Trafalgar Street, on the 13th November, 1845, upon which occasion nearly the whole adult population of the settlement dined together.

During the day effigies of the Governor and the two Clarks were paraded about the town in procession, and at night there was a grand auto-da-fé and display of fireworks, accompanied with tumultuous outbursts of applause from the adults and juveniles assembled.

Colonists of the present day, exercising the political privileges conferred by the Constitution Act, and enjoying the advantages and familiarised with the working of free institu-

I

tions established by constitutional government, can but very inadequately comprehend the nature and extent of the special grievances of the early settlers, an intimate knowledge of which is necessary to a proper understanding of the general and spontaneous outburst of enthusiasm evoked upon this occasion throughout the settlement—a simultaneous expression of the popular feeling of relief, that united all classes in one common bond. Perhaps some little allowance may be made for the extreme youth of the settlement. The country was new; experience had to be gained; all the surroundings were novel, inchoate and untried, and, insensibly re-acting upon the character of the people, possibly may have had the effect of rejuvenating this small section of Old England.

About this time my partner and I consented to join with three others in the building of a vessel of between thirty and forty tons burden.

It was proposed, when she was finished, to freight her with potatoes (our own produce) and sail to Tahiti, where it was understood a

A Fresh Start.

ready sale would be found for the vessel and cargo, at very remunerative prices. I understand my old acquaintance E. was the originator of the proposal, but it was cordially entered into by the others, as with his co-operation the scheme was feasible, and quite within our means to accomplish. Our own labour could supply all the timber required, the price of a few tons of potatoes sent to market from time to time would procure all the necessary iron work, and we had no doubt about being able to provide rigging, sails, and outfit by the time the hull was finished, and engaging a captain to navigate her, we constituting the crew, as in boating about the tidal creeks, and to and from the bays on the coast, we were all pretty well at home on salt water. On the passage from England it occurred to me that a knowledge of the ropes, and some little insight into, and experience of, a seaman's duty might be very useful should any untoward circumstances drive me to the necessity of working my passage back to the old country.

I therefore made my desire known to the

second mate, a young man about my own age, who kindly agreed to assist me all he could. From this time forth to the end of the voyage I regularly turned out at the appointed time, when it was his watch on deck, going aloft to help reef, when sail had to be shortened, and profiting all I could by the opportunities afforded, so that I was nearly half a sailor by the time we reached New Zealand. E. had visited Tahiti, and gave us a very favourable account of the country, and demonstrated to our entire satisfaction the many advantages it possessed over New Zealand, and quite enlisted our hearts and minds in the determination to do our utmost to carry out the project to a successful issue. The plan of precedure was to extend the building of the vessel over about twelve months, so as to carry on our cultivations simultaneously. I was to assist E. in the carpenter's work, while the others put in the crops, and at spare intervals cut planking, procure timbers, knees, etc.

E., when all was arranged, removed from Nelson to Riwaka with his wife and two daughters (the eldest having married and gone a Fresh Start. 117

to England the previous year), and built himself a house near a tidal creek, at the side of which it was intended to build the vessel, for the convenience of launching her. As I was to assist E. in the building of the vessel, and my house being too far from the work, it was arranged that I should reside with them, and give up my bachelor residence, to which I was very agreeable. I therefore, to turn my place to some account in forwarding the work in hand, arranged with a good sawyer in the valley to exchange my house and improvements for so many days' labour in sawing timber for the vessel, my late partner in agricultural pursuits acting as pitman, having had some previous experience at sawing.

A birch tree was selected, felled, and a keel of the required dimensions sawn and conveyed up the creek, and fixed on the stocks, with very lively feelings of satisfaction and rejoicing, as we now considered our project fairly commenced.

A day or two after procuring the keel, I and another of our party started down the creek in a small punt, to cut down a tree previously selected as being suitable for a stem, it having the required sweep, and being also accessible from the tide-way, whence it was our intention, after cutting off a suitable length, to tow it to its destination.

The tree was soon cut down, but as the flood spring-tide was running in fast, by the time we commenced the cross-cutting the water was just rippling over it, and before the work was finished it was nearly rippling over us. We had some difficulty in getting one end triced up to the stern of the punt, as, being black birch, its density made it almost as unmanageable as a large stone in the water; and when we fairly got under weigh, it hung suspended perpendicularly from the stern, and would have submerged the punt had we not kept well in the bows. We could not get it far up the creek on that tide, and it was several tides and with considerable difficulty that it was eventually got to the scene of operations, and then, being found too faulty for the purpose, it was abandoned, and a rimu one procured from the adjoining bush instead of it. A few weeks' steady labour completed

A Fresh Start.

the first section of the vessel, to the height of the floor timbers, when other equally important, though less agreeable work next claimed our attention. As there was a fine piece of bush just opposite to where the vessel was being built, and about an acre near the road that required very little clearing, and it being the time for potato planting, E. and I decided to appropriate and plant it forthwith.

The road from the valley turned at a right angle at this spot on to the plains, the bush being in the angle of the two roads, and enclosed by the ditch dug to form the roads. It was this corner of the bush having a frontage to each of the roads we were intent upon planting. I have been thus particular in describing the locality, on account of what occurred so soon after our beginning the vessel, which resulted in the abandonment of that enterprise.

In clearing the land, instead of burning the brushwood where it lay, as usual in such cases, we carried it to the margin of the clearing, and with it formed a temporary fence, the road ditch constituting a fence on the other two sides. As the planting of this small patch was soon finished, and there was some good flax-land close by, I began clearing a piece of it by firing it in several places, but E. expressed strong objection to the burning when he saw what I was doing, fearing the danger of the fire extending. I immediately extinguished, as I supposed, the fires I had lighted; but being land of a swampy character, but quite dry at that time of year, it burnt under the surface, and for a fortnight after was frequently breaking out in different places. And here I cannot help pausing to reflect what slight circumstances and trivial actions often influence our whole future destiny. If I had not kindled that fire, it is more than probable the vessel would have been built, and the future of myself and co-partners transferred to another country.

About a fortnight after the first starting of the fire, the brushwood fence was observed in a blaze. E. and I ran with buckets, and, with water from the ditch close by, soon got it under control, when I saw it break out in another place, and leaving E. to finish that

A Fresh Start.

which we had nearly subdued, I went to the new part attacked, which was at some distance, and nearest the ditch upon the other frontage from which I procured the water. I had been busily employed for about five minutes, when I observed the first fire blazing as furiously as at first, but E. was not to be seen. I immediately rushed to the spot, and was horrified at finding E. lying across a hollow, apparently dead, and dangerously near the burning fence. I moved him a short distance and shouted to a man who was working near, and with his assistance he was carried to the house, where all needful restoratives were tried, but without effect, as in falling across a hollow place in the ground his neck had been dislocated. This sad occurrence brought our ship-building venture to a premature termination.

One of our party was so bent upon obtaining a vessel of some kind, that he shortly after went to Nelson, and made arrangements for one to be built of about ten tons, and with which he traded between Nelson and Wellington for several years very successfully. Another apprenticed himself to a Nelson shipwright for two years, expecting by that time to acquire sufficient skill and knowledge of the business as would enable him to complete the vessel we had begun under such favourable auspices, the other partners agreeing to resign all interest in the work and materials to him.

I may add here that at the end of his two years' probation, though not succeeding to the extent anticipated, he did with the materials build a vessel of about half the tonnage of the one originally designed.

Being now the head of the household, I fell back into the old groove, and continued delving with the spade, and, having E.'s tools, occasionally repaired a boat, or did small jobs of carpentry for neighbours.

Mrs. E. informed me that some time before leaving Nelson, E. had agreed to buy a cow in milk, from a friend at the Waimea, and had paid part of the purchase money. Upon learning this, I at once went to the Waimea with the balance of the purchase money, obtained possession of the cow, and with a good deal

A Fresh Start.

of fatigue and difficulty succeeded in driving her over the ranges to the Riwaka, and her milk made a very satisfactory addition to the household comforts. Although we were not short of wheat, there was still the old difficulty of the grinding of it, which caused us to be too much limited to a potato diet, and to which a long experience had failed to reconcile me. The old hand-mill had given place to a water-power one, constructed entirely by one of the residents, a very intelligent, ingenious, and able workman, but from the machinery being nearly all of wood it was necessarily of low power, and, like another celebrated mill, " ground exceeding slow." I used often to take a bushel of wheat to the mill when I could get the night turn, and wait patiently all night while the flour slowly dribbled from the stones, carrying home the result about four o'clock in the morning. I had an idea that the mill-owner from prudential motives purposely reduced the speed upon these occasions, as it appeared to me to grind much faster in the day-time under his own superintendence.

In order to get some relief from this night watching, I upon one occasion sent two sacks of wheat to Nelson to be ground, anticipating in consequence to be relieved of all anxiety about flour for some time, but unfortunately the two bags of flour were lost after nearly reaching their destination. The boat being left in the creek unattended for a short time, the receding tide caused it to ground on the steep bank of the creek, and as the tide lowered the boat fell over, throwing all its contents into the rapid current, which swept everything out to sea.

Occasionally a party of Maories would arrive at the mill from Motueka, with wheat to be ground (for this was the only mill of the kind on our side of the bay), and during their stay would make it very lively for the mill-owner by their curiosity and inquisitiveness. They also invariably brought with them a large go-ashore, or three-legged pot, of the shape and size of the cauldron usually introduced in the witch scene in Macbeth, and so soon as there was sufficient flour available for the purpose, they would

A Fresh Start.

concoct a potfull of lilipee, as it was called, and, jabbering round it in a cluster, like flies at a sugar basin, each provided with a mussel-shell, would soon dispose of its contents.

Upon one occasion one of the Maories was squatting down in the mill near where the flour was falling from the stones, intently watching its accumulation, while his companions were busily engaged in lighting a fire and getting the pot under way. He, probably lost in a revery of speculation of the tightening process so near at hand, suddenly found the mill was capable of producing a tightening of another kind not anticipated or prepared for. The two ends of his blanket were caught, and drawn in by the cog-wheels in such a manner that he could not slip out of it, and could only call lustily for help, which was soon afforded. Half-a-dozen Maories rushed in, and, seizing hold of the large driving wheel, prevented its revolving by sheer physical strength, the wooden cogs, yielding to the strain, being stripped off the wheel, and their companion extricated from his dangerous position. I have previously referred to a contract that was taken by two of the settlers, first-rate bushmen, to procure a quantity of spars for a Nelson merchant; these were to be cut in one of the bays round the coast, and to be collected in a position convenient for shipment. As extra assistance was required for the latter condition, my partner and I, and another, a tall Scotchman, were engaged to help in this work.

The bush where they had been cut was at the head of a long shallow sandy bay about a mile from its entrance seaward. The sandy flat was bare at low water, except where intersected by narrow rivulets and creeks, but when the tide was in, was one large sheet of water to the margin of the bush, as there is a rise and fall at spring tides of from 12 to 15 feet in Blind Bay. The work we assisted at was wading at high water with the spars singly, which were from 60 to 80 feet long, a certain distance down the bay, to where there was sufficient depth of water to float a raft when constructed, whence the raft or rafts could be poled to near the entrance of the bay.

It was in March, and a very keen cold wind

A Fresh Start.

was blowing, when we were engaged in this work, wading to the waist and sometimes to the chin. As I could not swim at the time, I had to carefully follow down the margin of a channel as long as it continued in the right direction, but when it took a sharp turn, or was joined by another, it had to be crossed, which I managed by giving an onward impetus to the spar, and clinging to the end of it until the deep water was passed. The tall Scotchman attempted the passage of one of these channels by trying to walk on the spar, but not having received a gymnastic training his precipitate descent from the revolving log was as rapid as ludicrous.

Upon another occasion when we went down to help get them rolled up the bank above high water mark we all had a narrow escape from being drowned. The work was duly finished by dusk, but as we could not start until high water we had to wait until about 12 o'clock. Soon after the turn of the tide, we in our boat dropped down to the entrance with the current, which was already running out strong, when, on rounding a bluff point, we found a frightful surf breaking right across the outer entrance of the bay. We had to put about at once, but, with the strong tide running out, it was doubtful at one time whether we should be able to master it. The boat was a small one, with only two oars, which we durst not double bank, for fear of a thole pin breaking, when we should have been swept into the boiling surf in a very few minutes. After a hard struggle we succeeded in getting round the point and back to the starting place, when we hauled the boat upon the sandy beach above high water mark, and walked over the ranges, dropping down into Riwaka Valley just at daybreak, not having broken our fast since the previous morning's breakfast, as we had calculated upon getting back the same evening.

One of the residents of the valley was the owner of a bull that was the terror of the entire community, for, although reared in the place, it turned out a very savage animal. One day, being at work for a neighbour in the valley, I saw it swim the tideway, and rush bellowing towards the plains.

As our house was situated near the bend of

A Fresh Start.

the road, and having left Mrs. E. quite alone, I thought she might be caught unawares, and perhaps rushed by the savage brute, I therefore left my work and followed him at a respectful distance, and managed to get to the house unobserved.

In making an inspection of the premises, he took no account of fences, but just walked through them as if there were none, sending the rails flying right and left; after ripping some of the thatch off the roof of the cow-shed with his short straight horns, he strode across the potato plot, walking through the fence in another place, jumped across the ditch to the angle piece of bush-land where I had some pigstys, and began tearing the thatch off their roofs.

Annoyed at having so much damage done, and reasoning with myself that probably his pugnacity was chiefly due to his having everything his own way, and being accustomed to see every one fly before him, but that if he were boldly confronted he would probably fly in his turn, I without further reflection resolved to test the point. Seizing a broken adze, the handiest weapon at hand, I jumped across the ditch, and before he could recover from his astonishment at my presumption, dealt him what I thought was a terrific blow between the eyes, which simply produced a momentary shake of the head, as if a fly had annoyed him, and instead of rushing away to avoid a second blow, before I could repeat the dose, his forehead was against my chest impelling me rapidly rearward. The motion was so swift that I was carried about a dozen yards before losing my footing, and then fortunately finding myself alongside the ditch, I gave a rapid turn over into it, just in time to avoid a lunge. On emerging at the other side I observed him making desperate lunges at my cap, which had fallen off just as I slipped out of his way, and as he did not immediately recross the ditch, which could have been done in an instant, I was fortunate in his resting content with my representative.

Shortly after this he attacked and nearly killed a man in the valley, and the resident magistrate at Motucka ordered him to be shot.

A Fresh Start.

Just previous to this tussle with the bull I had a narrow escape from what might have proved a very ugly accident, though brought about in a rather ridiculous manner.

Being an early riser, it was my custom to light the fire, and put the kettle on in the morning, and to facilitate matters I usually provided some light sticks or red pine chips over-night, but upon the occasion referred to, this had been neglected.

As there were some red pine stumps just across the road, a few chips cut from which soon made a good fire, and not seeing the axe, I seized a mattock that was near the door, and rushed across to slice a few chips off one of the said stumps as quickly as possible. Now any bushman knows that the top of a sound red pine stump is nearly as hard and solid as a blacksmith's anvil, and if struck on the top with an axe anywhere but close to the outer edge, the axe will rebound with great force.

The mattock referred to was like a pick-axe, with one of its points flattened into an axe-shape for cutting roots, and either from its not being so handy, or so easily directed as an axe, or in my haste I was less careful, I had not time to consider, I struck a forcible but erring blow, and the same instant was laid flat on my back with a curious feeling about my nose; fortunately the pick end of the mattock happened to be too blunt to penetrate, and the cartilage of the nose proving an excellent buffer, no serious damage or disfigurement resulted from the concussion. While writhing and twisting from the first effect of the blow, I could not help feeling amused at the rapidity of the whole affair, as from my first seizing the mattock, striking the blow, getting felled myself, and returning to the house, barely occupied a minute.

About the end of the year 1847, we, that is, Mrs. E., the girls, and I, received an invitation to a supper and dancing party, given by some mutual friends in Nelson to commemorate some event. F., our former partner in the vessel, brought his schooner across the bay for us; the party was a very enjoyable one, dancing being kept up with great spirit until daylight.

F. and I and two or three other young men

then walked down the beach to the schooner, intending to turn in for an hour for two to sleep; on reaching the schooner we thought it absurd to go to bed and the sun shining brightly. For myself I can answer that in the cool fresh morning air, I did not feel the slightest symptom of fatigue, notwithstanding the night's dissipation, and on reaching the Waimea Road on our way back to town, I said to my companions that I should walk home, and accordingly started, and reached the banks of the Motueka River the same evening, and although there was a ferry-boat established at this time, the ferryman refused to put me across on account of the flooded state of the river. I had crossed the Wairau on a cart loaded with potatoes, after having tried to wade it in several places. The Moutere, usually a small river, gave me some trouble and risk from its swollen state, and having reached within two miles of home, I was annoyed at having to remain at Motueka until the morning.

A week or two after the foregoing some friends, residing about eight miles from Nelson, paid a special visit to the Riwaka, for the purpose of proposing that Mrs. E. and her daughters should remove from the Riwaka and go to reside with them; I was also included in the invitation. They had a very nice place, a number of cows, a team of working bullocks and plough, and all the conveniences and accessories of a dairy farm, and a good run for the cows in the neighbourhood. I considered it would be a beneficial change for Mrs. E. and the girls; and if after experience it did not please me, I should be free to begin some other career, which I was not inclined to under the existing circumstances. We could not attach much value to the house, sheds, fences, and other improvements, being merely squatters, for at first the house was only intended to serve for a temporary purpose, while the vessel was being built; but as I had parted with my own home just before her keel was laid, I afterwards extended the cultivations and improved the house.

Our arrangements were soon made for removing to the other side of the bay: a crop of wheat was growing, and I agreed with a neighbour

A Fresh Start.

to hand over to him the place as it stood, upon condition of his harvesting the corn, thrashing it, and delivering the produce upon the wharf at Nelson.

Arrived at our new home, I found its inmates constituted quite a small community, as besides its original owners, consisting of a Mr. W., his wife, and two sons, aged respectively about 16 and 18, and an old friend of the family (a most ingenious and clever artisan, and an indefatigable worker), there were now added a blacksmith (an old ' Indus ' acquaintance), a man from Nelson, a shoemaker by trade, his wife, and our party from the Riwaka. It was the most industrious hive of workers to be found anywhere, for wet weather or fine; there was appropriate work to do, and it was done.

The head matron of the establishment was a wonderfully active and energetic body, and ruled the house with such tact and good management that everything connected with the household, and its multifarious duties, worked with harmonious smoothness and regularity.

My first essay at pit sawing began a few days after arriving. Some additions to the house were rendered necessary by the recent enlargement of the family circle, a new dairy was also much needed, and as there was a bush close by, it was a simple matter to provide whatever timber was required.

But oh! my arms, shoulders, neck, and limbs generally! The only time they ceased aching was when I was actually at work, and I could not enjoy a night's rest until after about a week's practice at this new work.

I was pitman, and I think if one ache was more persistent and intrusive than another, it was in the back of the neck caused by looking upwards to watch the saw line, while the shoulders were bent. I had often seen quite young lads at this work and they appeared to work with the greatest ease and comfort; I had no idea of the tortures to which the neophyte was subjected upon initiation.

In a small valley upon the estate, a hand flour-mill similar to my old acquaintance of the Riwaka, was set up; but here the power of a

A Fresh Start. 137

small stream of water was utilised for turning it, and with a very large hopper for containing a good supply of grist, it continued its untiring course day and night, requiring very little attention, and supplying all the large household requirements.

Upon wet days the shoemaker worked at his trade; I assisted the blacksmith, who was quite a genius in his way. He had constructed a scarifier that was expected to do wonders in tearing the bulrush roots out of the swamp land, and was preparing the iron work for a saw mill, that I felt particular pleasure in forwarding as much as possible; while the others, all expert carpenters, would be busily engaged in the workshop upon some other parts of the machinery.

But the work that claimed particular attention at this time, and at which we were all continuously engaged in fine weather from "smiling morn to dewy eve," was the cutting a large ditch through a swamp for the purpose of draining and reclaiming a 50-acre section of land of which a lease with a purchasing clause had been taken. This was a very costly and laborious undertaking, but was absolutely necessary to render the land available for agricultural purposes.

Like the generality of swamps of this kind in New Zealand it was one mass of timber, the roots of an extinct forest, and the labour of chopping, and levering, and working in a mass of slough and water was of the most trying and exacting nature, and the progress of the work proportionately slow.

I continued at this work several months, and although it was intended that I should share equally with the rest in all of the advantages resulting from our united labour, I felt a strong desire for a change, and resolved to seek an early opportunity of carrying out my intention.

When the melancholy loss of my old friend occurred, I felt as keenly as my co-partners the disappointment and consequent failure of the vessel.

Previous to the proposal to build the vessel, I was fairly contented, but this project unsettled me, and having parted with my home, that had cost a severe struggle to found, had I

A Fresh Start. 139

been free to have followed my own inclinations, I would then have tried in some other sphere or occupation, to win a position or some more satisfactory measure of success than I could hope for by again beginning the delving in the Riwaka. The peculiar circumstances, however, in which I found myself placed precluded the taking of any steps, or forming any plans that would necessitate a removal from the valley for carrying them into execution, and as a consequence I had to fall back into the old groove, apparently for an indefinite period.

But circumstanced as I was now, I was free to choose and resolved to take a new departure. My old acquaintance, the ex-storekeeper of the valley store, was at this time in an office at Wellington, I therefore wrote requesting him to use his best endeavours to procure me a situation in some store or office (he knowing pretty well my capabilities) with as little delay as possible. By the next course of post I received the gratifying news that he had succeeded, and that I was to come to Wellington by the first opportunity. I had apprised my friends of my intentions, and I believe they were sincerely sorry at my determination to leave, and endeavoured to dissuade me from so doing, but my resolution was taken, and in a few days after the receipt of the Wellington letter I was on board the schooner of my friend F., that I have before referred to, and who at this time was a regular trader between Wellington and Nelson.

I landed in Wellington August 14th, 1848, my sole possession being a very large middy's chest, the size and weight of which might have conveyed the impression that it was well stocked with clothes, but appearances are often deceptive as in this *case*, as unfortunately for me it was quite empty.

I entertain a great regard for that old chest; in the process of various removals, and migrations from one province to another, and consequent disposal of household effects, it has been retained and is still in my possession. In a recent removal, and because of its capacity and apparent strength, it was proportionally honoured with an unlimited responsibility, and I regret to add its bottom

A Fresh Start. 141

fell out, but its merits insured it a speedy repair and re-instatement in the household.

My new employment was as book-keeper in a general store. There was also a salesman and porter, the latter a Maori, a native of Taranaki, very intelligent, and tolerably well educated; having lived with Europeans from his boyhood he was the most civilised native I had met. I found it very interesting listening to his stories of the doings of the natives prior to the arrival of the settlers. He was a lad at the time of the wreck of the 'Harriet' at Taranaki, and remembered the event quite well, and the massacre of all prisoners except Mrs. Guard, and for her possession there were several desperate encounters between rival parties. She was finally rescued by a vessel sent down expressly by the Sydney Government, and lived for many years afterwards in Queen Charlotte Sound.

Part of the plundered cargo of the vessel consisted of boxes of soap, which the Maories, though not liking its taste, firmly believed to be some kind of preserved food of the Pakehas, and taxed their ingenuity to discover the proper method of cooking it, but after roasting and boiling, failing to make it more palatable, they were obliged reluctantly to give it up.

A quantity of silver coinage also fell into their hands, and not having any other use for it, they utilised it for draughtsmen, a game at which they are great adepts.

Having being so long accustomed to laborious work in the open air, and enjoying the most robust health, I was apprehensive that such a radical change from a very active to a sedentary occupation and comparative confinement might injuriously affect it, so resolved to continue my habit of early rising, and used to take long walks before business hours commenced. In pursuance of this plan I usually found the store still unopened on my return, and considering it was time to begin preparations for business, and feeling some responsibility in the matter, I generally opened the store, and swept it out before my co-partner appeared on the scene.

Upon one occasion I had opened and swept the store as usual, and it being a damp morning I had thrown down a quantity of

A Fresh Start. 143

sawdust, which was kept on the premises for the purpose; when my companion appeared, for some reason that I do not remember, he did not approve of the sawdust, and proceeded leisurely to sweep it off again. I thought if he had opened the store and swept it, which he was expected to do every morning, he might have used sawdust or not unquestioned by me, but as I had voluntarily undertaken this work in his absence, I could not endure what I foolishly perhaps considered was an impertinent interference, and at once stepped across to take the broom from him. A desperate struggle ensued; a stranger would have probably thought we were fairly matched in weight and stature for a pugilistic encounter, but I soon discovered the error; the rapidity with which the blows were rained upon my face and head generally, without my seeming to get a chance of guarding or retaliating very *forcibly* convinced me I had made a *striking* mistake, and I was only saved from an ignominious defeat by the timely intervention of a third party.

I had no idea of entering upon such an

encounter, but a moment's reflection would have suggested the very probable result of two opposing forces coming into collision. I may note here that previous to this affair we had been on the most friendly terms, and I am also pleased to record that from that time to the present we have remained staunch friends. Some time afterwards, when I had started a business on my own account, I was glad of the chance of having his ability and valuable business knowledge enlisted in my service; he lived with me nearly two years and only left to go into business for himself. It was shortly after my settling in Wellington, on October 16th, 1848, that the first serious earthquakes in New Zealand occurred, and which caused very general consternation and alarm, as it was thought by many to be the precursor of more violent convulsions. A number of settlers in a panic sold off their possessions at a great sacrifice, and took passages in the 'Sabraon,' the only ship that happened to be in the harbour at the time, but by a singular fatality, those fleeing from earthquakes were subjected to shipwreck, as the vessel was wrecked near the entrance of harbour shortly after leaving her anchorage, and the majority of the passengers, fugitives they might be called, finding that fate appeared to be arrayed against their quitting the country, resolved to remain and take their chance with their fellow colonists.

I remember when the earthquake occurred the weather was very wet and stormy, and had been for the two preceding days; a hurricane of wind and an almost ceaseless downpour of rain flooding the streets and levelling fences in various parts of the town. When I retired to rest on Sunday night, the 15th, there was no abatement of the storm, and my first impression upon being awakened by the unusual vibration was, that it was caused by a more than ordinary violent gust of wind, and that the building was going to collapse, but in an instant I realised its true cause.

Sleeping in the upper part of a store adjoining the main building, I had often noticed with a critical eye the bad workmanship of the roof, and sometimes when the wind was blowing as it only can blow in Wellington, I was afraid it would be carried clean away; but now with an earthquake superadded it may be taken for granted that I was uncommonly nimble in reaching and opening the outer door.

The storm still raged without, but not caring to face the wind and rain in such light attire, I stood just within the shelter of the passage, ready for a spring when the crash came which I was momentarily expecting. After an interval of eight or ten minutes, the shocks not being repeated, and feeling cooler and calmer, I ventured to retire to bed once more, though still very sceptical as to the safety of the building.

On entering the store soon after daylight a frightful scene of wreck and breakage presented itself, the shelves were nearly cleared of all their long array of bottles, the floor being covered with the *débris* of what had been bottled fruits, pickles, salad oil, etc. etc., and a large tank that contained about two hogsheads of whale oil, and which had been recently filled, had been hurled from its usual position to the opposite side of the store, and about half its contents spilt in its flight.

After throwing down sundry bags of sawdust, and working vigorously with barrows and shovels, by mid-day the wreck was cleared away, and something like order once more restored, when our attention was called to the dangerous state of one of the chimneys. The portion that projected above the roof, about six feet, had been broken off near the roof, and turned round on the stack without being thrown down, thus indicating a rotatory as well as an undulating motion. A slight tremor of the earth continued at short intervals during the day and night, preceded by a low rumbling but unmistakable sound.

At noon on Tuesday, the 17th, a customer was settling an account at the store, and I was just handing him the receipt, and remarking about the earthquake and its effects, when a violent shock occurred that caused us both to rush out of the store from its violence; his dray and team of bullocks which had been left standing in front of the store, had gone tearing down the inclined street, the animals having been frightened by the strange movement of the earth. Upon my returning to the desk where I had been writing, I found the floor strewn with loaves of sugar, and the desk much indented by their falling upon it from the top shelves. All the bottles and goods on the lower shelves had been made secure by passing wire along the front of them, but the heavy goods upon the top shelves had been thought quite safe. Brick walls and chimnies, that had only been partially damaged, were mostly shaken down by this one.

The Barrack Master of the 65th Regiment and his two children were killed at this time; he had been walking about the town with his children, surveying the mischief that had resulted from the shocks on Monday, when a large brick wall near which they were standing when the second shock occurred, fell upon them, killing them instantly.

On Friday, the 20th, about 5 A.M., occurred the third violent shock of the series, for during the intermediate time there had been

A Fresh Start.   149

a constant repetition of slight tremors, so that the earth was scarcly quiescent the whole time.

This nearly completed the destruction of everything breakable. While hastily dressing myself I heard the store door violently slammed with the wind; wondering at its being open so early, I went down to secure it, and found the violence of the shock had caused the lock to slip out of the fastening, and the lock had to be turned back, unlocked in fact, before the door could be re-closed.

There was great commotion in the street, some rushing about, and others standing in groups detailing their experiences and losses; I soon sallied forth to ascertain what further damages had resulted. At one of the hotels some very large ornamental casks, ranged upon a stand at the back of the bar, were thrown clean over the counter to the front of the bar. I saw Mr. W. B. Rhodes riding furiously towards the barracks for a company of soldiers, I was informed, to protect his bonded stores, a two-storyed brick building, which was completely wrecked with its contents; cases of brandy, wine, champagne, etc. intermixed with bricks and timber, forming one promiscuous heap of ruins.

Walking along Lambton Quay I passed an hotel kept by a Prussian named Albert Hesse, where the breakage and loss during the week had been so great, that I suppose he thought he might as well distribute the balance of it gratis, and even at that early hour there were plenty of thirsty souls ready to take advantage of his liberality.

Continuing my stroll as far as a dispensary called Medical Hall, I saw a woman rush from the building enveloped in a blanket, as it was supposed the place was on fire ; but all danger from this cause was soon removed.

It was supposed to have originated from the breaking of some bottles containing Aquafortis, or some other corrosive chemicals.

If the proverbial bull had had the run of the china and crockery-ware shops, I am sure the unfortunate owners of the latter would not have had to deplore such an amount of breakage as resulted to their particular stocks from this week of earthquakes.

A Fresh Start.

At the time of the recall of Governor Fitzroy, and the appointment of Sir G. Grey, the latter had the onerous task of quelling the native disturbances that were becoming very serious in the neighbourhood of Auckland and the Bay of Islands.

These were scarcely got well under when Rauparaha and Ranghiaita commenced near Wellington, and a good deal of fighting took place in the Upper Hutt, and a good many lives were lost before they were thoroughly subdued.

But the death of Ranghiaita and the clever capture of Rauparaha by Sir G. Grey were primarily conducive to this result.

Rauparaha was kept a prisoner on board one of the men-of-war, the 'Caliope' I think, until he died.

Upon the vessel visiting Nelson, I and several others went on board to see the redoubtable old savage; he was in a compartment on deck when I saw him, and was wearing the uniform of a naval officer. He resented being subjected to the inspection of strangers, and upon our approaching near, demanded to know, in a defiant tone, "what we came to stare at."

Sir G. Grey's success in intimidating and subduing the natives gained for him great *éclat* with the settlers, and also the Home Government, presuming upon which he drew largely upon the English Treasury; but his autocratic and despotic measures soon changed the current of public opinion in New Zealand.

A Constitutional Society was formed at Wellington, and included among the members all its leading settlers.

The 'Wellington Independent' was started for the dissemination of constitutional politics, and to aid the cause generally of the settlers in their efforts to obtain a more liberal form of Government. As all the talent of the settlement was at its command, the political warfare was carried on with great vigour, and continued unabated, until the Constitution Act conferred representative institutions upon the colony.

The 'Wellington Spectator' very feebly endeavoured to defend the Governor, his nominees, and measures. Its proprietor and editor was dubbed 'Robert the Scribe' in a clever *jeu d'esprit* called the 'Chaldean Manuscript," written in an oriental style, well sustained, which passed in review in a very humorous manner all connected with the Nominee Council.

CHAPTER VII.

DECIDEDLY NAUTICAL.

Early in 1849 information reached Wellington that the preliminaries were all arranged for the establishing of a Church of England Settlement in New Zealand, to be called " Canterbury." About June Captain Thomas, with a strong party of surveyors, mechanics, and labourers, the latter chiefly Maories, started from Wellington to proceed to Port Cooper, the present Port Lyttelton, to prepare for the arrival of the settlers.

I resolved to start a small business in the new settlement about the end of the year, and soon had the satisfaction of knowing that my employer would assist me with stores and liberal credit if I could manage to provide a suitable building in which to begin business.

This I considered quite within my means to accomplish. As timber was cheap in Nelson, I decided to go there and frame the building myself; and when everything was ready, my old friend F. agreed to make a trading trip to Port Cooper, giving my traps and myself a passage down. F. was still a regular trader between Wellington and Nelson, and at this time was also the owner of a cutter, about the same burden as the schooner—namely, ten tons. The schooner was at this time engaged in what was called the Wairau trade—that is, conveying sheep and wool from the Wairau (Marlborough) to Wellington, loading back with stores, etc.

In the present day, with large coastal steamers running almost daily between the settlements, it may excite a smile to hear of such cockle-shells as the foregoing performing the same voyages, and literally feeling their way into the harbours on the darkest nights, as there were no lighthouses or beacons in those days to guide the mariner; and the intercommunication between the settlements was so limited, that such small craft, with the occasional visit from an Australian trader, sufficed for its requirements.

The cutter was under charter to proceed to Poverty Bay, for a cargo of maize I believe, about the time that I wished to go to Nelson to make a start of my new venture, so I had to await her return from the East Coast. Unfortunately, owing to baffling winds, gales, loss of sails, and various casualties, the cutter was absent upon this trip nearly two months; no uncommon occurrence with small craft trading on the East Coast in those days. It bore a bad reputation for sailing vessels, being so exposed, and a lee-shore with the prevailing strong winds; but as Wellington drew her chief supplies of produce, such as maize, pigs, potatoes, etc., from thence, the small coasters were the only medium for its conveyance to a market. As Poverty Bay was the chief *entrepôt* of this trade its name appeared a misnomer. There was a story current in Wellington of a confiding East-Coaster having sent a cargo of maize and pigs to a Wellington agent for sale and returns; and after vainly writing and waiting for a long time for account sales and remittance

Decidedly Nautical. 157

of proceeds, was at last informed that the pigs ate all the maize and then bolted into the bush, and a request was made for payment of rather a heavy bill of charges incurred.

A few days after the arrival of the cutter from the East Coast a start was made for Nelson, where I arrived early in September; and the timber having been purchased and collected beforehand, I at once began the framing of the house. F. had a cargo of barley to carry to Wellington, and expected to be back in Nelson in about a fortnight or three weeks, by which time I should have completed the house as far as was possible until it was erected.

Just before the cutter sailed news was brought to Nelson that F.'s schooner had been totally wrecked on the bar, at the mouth of the Wairau river. This was a serious and total loss, as there was no insurance on vessel or cargo; indeed, no one thought of such a thing at that time; I do not recollect if there were any marine insurance agencies then in the colony, but to the best of my belief there were none.

The truth of the old adage that misfortune seldom comes singly was forcibly verified a few days after the foregoing. About four or five days after F. had started with the cutter bound for Wellington, intending to call in at the Wairau on his return, to recover anything belonging to the schooner that might be useful or of value, he re-appeared in Nelson, and reported having left the cutter a partial wreck in Port Gore, an inlet near the Sound, and about eighty miles from Nelson. He had come alone that distance in the cutter's dingy; it being too small to carry two, he had left his man in charge of the wreck and cargo. It was a singular chance that this misfortune was primarily due to F. having taken extra precautions, induced by the recent loss of the schooner, and happened in this way, as told me by F. immediately after its occurrence. After leaving the French Pass, and getting well into the Straits with a fair wind, but blowing strong from the north-west, and evening just closing in, he calculated upon being at Wellington Heads about midnight, weather thick and squally, no moon, and the

Decidedly Nautical. 159

wind, though a fair one through the Straits, would be, in coasters' phraseology, a dead muzzler at the Heads. He knew from a lengthened experience the exact position in all its bearings, and under similar circumstances had always kept manfully on; but upon this occasion, with Port Gore under his lee, he resolved to run in and anchor under the shelter of the high land on the north shore until daylight, and then resume his voyage.

When daylight came the wind had died away, and to a practised eye there were unmistakable indications of a strong breeze coming up from the south-west. A heavy swell began to roll in, and it being very deep water a short distance from shore all round this part of the coast, there was about thirty fathom of chain out, to get in which would occupy considerable time; the cable was therefore buoyed, and they stood by to slip it so soon as the breeze came. The swell continued to increase, and with the cable payed out to the bare end, they were waiting in anxious expectancy for the wished-for wind.

At last a ripple was observed on the water

steadily approaching, and presently all sail was got on the cutter, the cable slipped, and they were speeding thankfully away on the starboard tack, and on the next board they would be able to lay right out. The breeze proved to be one of those fitful gusts that often precede a storm; before they could go about it fell dead calm, and having parted with their ground-tackle they were at the mercy of the heavy swell, which very soon hove them ashore on a rocky strand.

A hole was soon knocked in her bows, and she filled and grounded, with the deck just awash. If her cargo had not been grain she would have been safe from further damage, and they would have wisely left her until calm weather; but knowing that the swelling of the grain would soon burst her asunder, they bent all their energies to get it out of her on the falling tide, notwithstanding the difficulty of working with such a swell rolling in and continually breaking over them. At last, after incredible labour, and working for the most part under water, they had the melancholy satisfaction of knowing she was safe from the foregoing danger, from the number of bags of barley hoisted out of her; and when the weather moderated F. started upon his venturesome voyage of eighty miles in the dingy, a boat about eight feet long, two and a-half beam, and say eighteen inches deep, and usually stowed over the hatches of the cutter. Being fortunately favoured with fine calm weather, he reached Nelson on the morning of the second day.

From the account I received of the extent of the damage, I judged that with a blanket, a sheet of zinc, and a bucket of tar, she might be temporarily patched to enable her to be brought to Nelson for further repairs. Accordingly these were procured in the course of the day, and with a few friends, volunteers, we prepared to start at high water the same night for the scene of the wreck. An old resident of Queen Charlotte Sound, named Arthur Emsley, was in Nelson at the time, and being ready to start home we arranged to go in company, he kindly offering some three or four of our party room in his whale boat.

We started about twelve o'clock, dropping

down the harbour with the ebb-tide, weather looking rather threatening; and we had not proceeded far along the outside of the Boulder Bank when it came on to blow hard from the southward, obliging us to put into Shroeder's Mistake, now called Cable Bay. We were detained here wind-bound the whole of that day and night and the following morning. Although there was no change in the weather, and a very heavy sea outside, Emsley proposed our making a push for the Croiselles, stating that we might be detained a week, and that Captain McClaren, an old friend of his, was living there, who would entertain us with better fare, and more comfortable quarters, than sand-piper soup without salt and camping on the beach.

Accordingly another start was made under sail, and by short boards we fetched pretty well up to the south point when masts were unshipped and we had to bend to the oars with a will.

The sea was terrific rounding the point, and until we were well inside the Croiselles. I was pulling the stroke oar, Emsley was steering, and at times the boat seemed so nearly poised on end that I thought it was only by retaining a firm grip of the long steer oar he was enabled to maintain his standing, and at times almost horizontal position. It was a great relief to both mind and arms, after a long and laborious pull, when we at last shot into smooth water.

Captain McClaren was rejoiced to see Emsley his old friend and comrade in many a whale chase of former times; we also received from him a very hospitable reception; if the fatted calf was not killed for our especial behoof, the fat pig was, and all the resources of the establishment were placed at our disposal.

The house was very large, with a thatched roof, from the rafters of which depended hams, sides of bacon, dried fish, bunches of herbs, and bundles of unthrashed vegetable seeds of various kinds. One end of the building was nearly monopolized by a most capacious fireplace, the fire in which was never extinguished, it being part of the duty of certain swarthy vestals to keep it well supplied with fuel Adjoining the house was a well stocked garden and orchard that was nearly occupied by peach-trees, and near the beach a well-appointed whale boat, housed from the sun and wind.

Everything in and about the place gave evidence of careful forethought, and good management.

At one end of the building two rooms were partitioned off, one of which I had the privilege of inspecting; it was furnished in a style that would certainly have gladdened the heart of a dealer in old curiosities. There were antique bureaus, quaint old-fashioned circular mirrors, cunningly contrived lockers, and straight-backed chairs, whose ancient quaintness and old world associations contrasted curiously with their present surroundings, and conveyed the impression that various ships' cabins had been requisitioned for contributions; or a speculative mind might have woven a romance of rapine and plunder, and imagined that here was collected the spoils of wrecks, or various buccaneering exploits, and that the numerous drawers were filled with doubloons and Spanish gold and silver plate, did not the urbanity and peaceful character of the proprietor forbid such a conclusion.

Decidedly Nautical.

Here the Captain had lived in patriarchal simplicity for many years, rarely quitting his retirement, and seldom having an opportunity of exercising hospitality towards visitors as upon the occasion of our arrival.

Emsley and he, though comrades in the old whaling days, had not met until the present occasion for fifteen years; and when after refreshments, and a stroll round the premises, and its various conveniences and advantages dilated upon and discussed, with the frankness and pleasure old friends find in exchanging ideas, they re-entered the house and sat down for a quiet chat about old times; and it is my belief that they neither moved from their seats nor ceased talking until breakfast time next morning.

One by one in the course of the evening our party stretched themselves on the floor, and were soon fast asleep, until at last from very weariness I was fain to do likewise, though I had been greatly interested in the ceaseless round of incident and adventure that was poured out by those two untiring and loquacious old cronies.

Sometime in the middle of the night I awoke and heard that "Stokes was last seen standing in the bow of the boat with harpoon poised ready to strike, when the fluke of the whale cut the bows of the boat clean off, and the rest found themselves struggling in the water."

After a detention of three days the weather moderated sufficiently for us to make a start on the morning of the fourth day.

We left our hospitable quarters about 3 A.M., in order to get through the French Pass at the top of high water, and so to carry the ebb tide with us nearly the remainder of the journey.

There was a light wind from the south-east, but smooth water all through the Pass; we pulled with a will, the boat going lightly off the oars in the strong ebb tide, which runs like a mill-race for about ten miles of the Pass, and reached the wreck at noon that day, being nearly a week after starting from Nelson.

Here we parted from our kind and pleasant companion Emsley, who continued his course alone, and was soon lost to sight on rounding Jackson's Head, his residence being in Ship's Cove, in the sound, almost in a bee line from where the wreck lay, but separated by the width of the bay and a lofty precipitous range of hills which terminated at Jackson's Head, whence a reef of rocks extend some distance seaward off the northern entrance to the sound.

Our party lost no time in getting a warp fast to the cutter and towing her to the head of the bay, where she was grounded on a sandy beach.

As she floated with her deck level with the water, this was a dead pull for about three hours; we found she had sustained more damage than was at first supposed, probably the result of the heavy weather that had detained us on the passage down, rendering temporary repairs out of the question.

The only course open for adoption was soon decided upon.

F. was aware that four shipwrights were at that time engaged building a small vessel at the head of the sou'-west arm of the sound, then known as Waitohi, now called Picton, and it was arranged that F. and I should be landed on the other side of the bay, and that we should walk over the range, drop down upon Emsley's place, who would have reached home before our arrival, borrow his boat and start at once for the Waitohi to bring back the shipwrights.

After landing us two the rest were to await our return, which, if unsuccessful in obtaining the shipwrights, would be by the same route over the hill, upon the summit of which we were to light a fire as a signal for the boat to fetch us across the bay; but if satisfactory arrangements were made with the shipwrights, we were certain they would have a boat for the conveyance of their tools, provisions, etc.; in such case we should be with them, and we expected to be back in either case by the evening of the following day.

In pursuance of this plan F. and I were landed on the southern side of Port Gore, and about six o'clock surprised Emsley by dropping as it were from the clouds upon his domicile in Ship's Cove.

He was just preparing his evening meal, and a share of the tea and damper was gratefully accepted, as we had only had a crust since our very early breakfast in the Croiselles.

The position of affairs was soon explained, and the loan of the boat readily granted, and refreshments concluded we started on our midnight cruise.

Emsley said it was a long pull and would take us till nine or ten next morning, pulling hard all the time, and advised our stopping for the night at what he called Maori kaik, which we should find just before turning up the sou'-west arm, and ought to reach it about twelve o'clock; and do the remainder of the journey, about twenty miles, next day.

The boat we borrowed was a five-oared whale-boat, and, after about four hours' pulling, it went very heavily and sluggishly, and we did not get along very fast; besides, our long day's unusual exertions began to tell upon both of us, and we strained our eyes to the utmost to discover through the gloom some faint vestige of the Maori kaik.

As hitherto we had been pulling from point to point across what appeared in the dark (for there was no moon) deep bays, we were apprehensive of passing our wished-for resting-place, and now began skirting the land with the intention of stopping at the first bit of beach that appeared, thus lengthening our route without obtaining the wished-for chance of landing, as the lofty hills seemed to rise sheer out of the water.

At last, about midnight, as near as I could judge, we came upon a bit of sandy beach, and after making the boat fast to one of the oars, forced at an angle into the sand, the yelping of dogs apprised us that here was the veritable Maori kaik we had been so long in search of.

A couple of Maories soon appeared, whom we accompanied to their wharé, but its numerous recumbent forms, and stifling atmosphere, decided us to prefer a shakedown on the boat's sail to such unsavoury quarters; we therefore returned to the boat, and were asleep almost before getting comfortably settled down.

I awoke soon after day-break and discovered that I had been reposing in about six inches of water, the boat (being a heavy one, we had not been able to draw her up on the beach) having leaked during the night, but I was so thoroughly worn out with fatigue that it had not disturbed me.

As action appeared to be the best antidote for stiffness, and as we had no provisions, therefore no time to be lost in getting breakfast, we were soon afloat once more.

As if to tax our strength and temper to the utmost the wind continued from the sou'-west, and freshened to a stiff breeze as the day wore on, causing a nasty chopping sea, and retarding our progress so much that it was two o'clock P.M. when we reached our destination, completely worn out with our great exertions and want of food. There were four men engaged upon a vessel of about fifteen tons; she was, when finished and launched, known as the ' Phœbe '.

It was soon arranged with them to undertake the repairs of the cutter, and after a refreshing meal off damper, wild pork, and tea, we turned into two of their bunks for a a couple of hours' sleep, while the carpenters looked up their tools, provisions, etc., they promising to rouse us at the last moment, when everything was ready for a start.

About six o'clock we were awakened from a refreshing sleep by the announcement that all was ready, and that with the fine fresh fair wind then blowing, we should round Jackson's Head by midnight.

As the carpenters preferred their own boat, we embarked with them, taking the whale boat in tow, and having nothing to do but recline at mine ease I experienced an exquisite sense of satisfaction and relief, in bowling along before a fresh breeze over the same route that had taxed our strength almost past endurance.

I had leisure to note that the carpenters had provided themselves with pit-saws, American felling axes, a small portable forge, a few bars of iron, and a bag of charcoal, besides several guns, and a couple of dogs for pig hunting; as in the execution of a job of this kind, upon a wild part of the coast, it was necessary to be prepared to improvise upon the spot everything that was required, from sawing the planking to forging a bolt; this also necessitated a certain versatility of resources and skill on the part of the operatives, that nothing but the exigencies of colonial life could develope.

I think it may be safely asserted, without fear of contradiction, that all who have achieved any measure of success in the colonies have been pre-eminently self-reliant men, though it is very probable that previous to emigrating dependence and vacillation were the chief characteristics of many, until new circumstances and new wants brought out this previously dormant trait in their characters.

The carpenters had correctly estimated the time required for the trip. About eleven o'clock Ship's Cove was reached, where we disengaged from the whale boat, and hauled her well up on the beach, having to disturb Emsley from his sleep, to apprise and thank him for the loan of her. After rounding Jackson's Head sail had to be taken in, as the wind drew right out of the bay; but four strong men at the oars, and the young flood tide, soon swept her up the bay to where the cutter lay aground, and the remainder of our party were encamped.

The first business of the morning was to assist the carpenters in removing the cutter above high water mark; this was rendered comparatively easy by the carpenters having been astir very early, and succeeding in getting skids under her keel before the tide fell; and our party, during the absence of F. and I, having recovered the anchor and chain that had been buoyed, it was of great service for a purchase in moving her up the inclined beach. The extent of the damage was such as to require new planking from the keel to the bilge pieces; the forefoot and keel were also much chafed with the friction on the stony beach, and probably when stripped some new timbers would be required.

The price for the repairs having been arranged, and the probable time stated— namely, three weeks—in which to effect them, we deemed it prudent to hasten our departure for Nelson, as the provisions were nearly exhausted. We were fortunately favoured with fine settled weather, and arrived at Nelson on the eve of the second day.

CHAPTER VIII.

DOWN SOUTH.

As F. intended making the previously projected trip down south when the cutter was again ready for sea, I set to with a will to complete the framing of the house that had been interrupted by recent events. It was soon completed, and I was ready to accompany F. and his man to Port Gore to bring up the cutter, as I knew he depended upon my assistance. It was not that my help was needed for working the cutter, as F. and his mate usually worked her without other assistance ; but it was a long and continuous pull down for two men, whereas a third man afforded a spell at intervals, and left one free to steer. Accordingly, about the time it was expected the cutter would be ready, we started from Nelson, taking with us a hundred-pound bag of flour, a small side of bacon, some tea and sugar, and a coil of rope for a new main sheet and peak halliards.

As usual, we started about midnight, to suit the tide, and have daylight for going through the pass; besides, we could generally depend upon the land breeze at night for dropping down the bay. We reached Port Gore the following evening, and were disappointed at finding that, owing to a good deal of wet weather and other causes, the repairs were not completed, and the carpenters were nearly run out of provisions, and it was nearly eight days before everything was taut and shipshape, by which time a clean sweep had been made of everything eatable.

We were to start at high water on Friday afternoon, and during the morning an excursion was made into the bush and a wild pig captured, one hind-quarter of which was appropriated to provisioning the vessel for the voyage to Nelson. As there was not a scrap of anything eatable but the pork, I filled a couple of empty potato kits with oysters, which were plentiful, and easily procured at low water, thinking they would be a useful addition to our limited fare. Soon after high water we stood down the bay, weather squally and threatening, and a head wind outside, but we hoped to be able to beat up to the Pass, and get through at high water in the morning.

On getting out of the land-locked bay we found it was blowing very hard outside, which made us regret not having taken in two or three tons more ballast. We also found the new peak halliards would not work freely, the rope being rather too large for the blocks, so that at critical moments when it was let go the peak of the sail did not come down, and F., who was steering, had to jam her up in the wind to prevent a capsize.

It was very dark, and we had been tacking to and fro in the Pass for about three hours, when from the outline of the hills F. judged we must be near a small bight called Catherine Cove, where we could anchor until daylight, and sufficiently near the narrows for us to get through at dead low water, instead of at high water as we first expected.

We had a Maorie passenger on board, and

F., supposing his sight, trained and accustomed to the appearance of the land at night, could be better depended on, posted him in the bows to keep a sharp look out as we neared the land. We were heading for shore on the starboard tack, and had entered the belt of almost impenetrable gloom that the high land threw for some distance over the water, and were all anxiously peering ahead when the Maorie gave the signal to go about, but it was too late, and a violent concussion followed. All sail was let go by the run ; we had run stem on to the almost perpendicular shore, and rebounded again a few yards from it with the shock. F. jumped down below, and after a short interval reported that she was all right, and not making any water, and ordered the jib to be run up to pay her head off shore ; but to do this we found it necessary to get on shore to clear it, as in lowering it had got entangled round a projecting rock. While this was being done F. discovered that the bottom rudder iron was carried away. This was temporarily righted by passing the bight of a rope round it, and she was soon driving through the water on the other tack as if nothing had happened. We surmised that the false keel was gone, and in driving on end had started the rudder, as so much of the original keel had been cut away that the bottom of the rudder was nearly level with the lower edge of the false keel. There was also something wrong about the cut-water that we could not make out in the darkness, causing an unusual commotion and noise as she surged through the water, and a phosphorescent column thrown up like the spouting of a mimic whale.

In this comparatively crippled state we were obliged to tack off and on for the rest of the night, and when daylight enabled us to distinguish the entrance to the small cove, we ran in and anchored close in shore, intending to lay her aground and overhaul the damages sustained after taking a few hours sleep, of which we were in much need.

It did not appear that I had been long asleep when I was awakened by the rapid paying out of the cable, and F. calling for us to turn out sharp. When I got on deck I found the cutter had drifted a short distance from shore, and was immediately in twenty fathom water, and had lost the shelter from the wind previously afforded by the high land. This was a very awkward state of affairs, as with all the cable payed out we were riding nearly over the anchor, and exposed to the full force of the blast, which struck the water just ahead of us, momentarily smoothing it down into widening circles of mist and spray, and then the cutter would jerk and reel, yielding to each violent gust some further portion of the coveted distance from shore. The inlet stretched away for about a mile to leeward, where the sea was breaking upon a rocky shore, and where it seemed we should find ourselves before many hours had passed. There was a small stream kedge below, so the mainsheet and peak halliards were unrove and bent on to it, being an entire coil of inch manilla. This was thrown overboard, with the hope that if she dragged, it and the anchor would bring her up when in shallower water before reaching the breakers. During the day a small schooner ran in for shelter, and brought up where we had originally anchored, and lay quite calm and secure in smooth and shallow water under the lee of the high land. Those on board, I have no doubt, wondered at the position we appeared to have chosen.

The quarter of pork which had been slung over the stern was lost when we ran on shore or some time during the night, so there only remained the two kits of oysters for the sustenance of four men, and if we succeeded in riding out the gale there was little probability of our getting to Nelson in less than two days, as there would be the delay of one, perhaps two tides, to examine the vessel and do what might be found necessary before continuing the voyage. Under these circumstances it was very tantalising to be so near assistance without the power of obtaining it or making known our critical position.

About 4 o'clock P.M. the ground-tackle yielded, and away we drifted before the tempest, our only chance of safety now depending upon the anchor and kedge being strong enough to resist the strain and bringing her up when in shallow water, which, fortunately, was the case, but only just in time, as her stern was only a few yards from the surf. As day declined the wind lulled, and next morning (Sunday) was a beautifully calm sunny morning. We lost no time in tripping the anchors and sailing to the upper end of the bight, and as the tide was falling, running her on to the sandy beach. We were not surprised to find the schooner gone, as we expected she would get away as soon as the weather moderated.

The cause of the surging at the bows was soon apparent. At Port Gore a new forefoot had been spliced on to the stem and false keel; the latter was gone, as we had surmised, and the forefoot had slewed round upon the one remaining bolt across and at right angles with the stem.

This was soon knocked into its place and spiked, the keel of the rudder temporarily secured, and as her bottom had sustained no damage, we were ready to start again as soon as the tide made sufficiently to float her.

As we were only a short distance from the Pass, we were enabled to get through by the same tide, but from calm and baffling winds it was Tuesday afternoon before we arrived nearly famished at Nelson.

About a week after this chapter of accidents we were loaded and ready to start for Port Cooper, the cargo consisting of flour, bacon, and my horse, with a few extra hundred feet of timber to fill up.

I was proceeding down the beach to the Custom-house to clear the vessel when I was seized with a severe pain in my left side; thinking it would pass off, if I moderated my pace, I continued on my errand, but instead of getting easier it increased until I was scarcely able to respire, and was obliged to lie down in a timber yard.

From thence I was conveyed back to town and a doctor summoned, who pronounced my ailment to be acute inflammation; a copious bleeding and a blister followed; it was short and sharp, for in a few days I was able to go on board the cutter which was waiting for me, feeling rather feeble but fairly progressing.

I concluded this short bout of illness was the result and sequel of the night I slept in the leaky boat when pulling through the Sound.

We had a fair wind through the straits and

were off the Kaikoras when we caught it thick and strong from the sou'-west.

After battling with it all night and making no headway, and there being no signs of its moderating, and the cutter leaking a great deal in her top sides as she lay over while close hauled, F. decided to run back to Wellington while he could insure daylight to make the heads.

The cutter was a capital sea-boat, and I had every confidence in the skill and judgment of F. who kept unwearied charge of the helm.

Our small craft seemed no bigger than one of the numerous sea-birds screeching around us, in contrast with the mighty sea that was running, and is invariably found across the entrance to the straits between Capes Campbell and Palliser, after a twelve hours' gale from the southward; but we careered along in gallant style, topping the swell as buoyantly as the gulls, and made very pleasant weather of it. We were just sufficiently laden to make her staunch and firm under the canvas carried, which was a storm jib, staysail, and single reef in the mainsail, and I should have enjoyed it much if her head had been pointing south instead of north.

As F.'s coasting experience had hitherto been limited to the straits north of Wellington, this was the first occasion of his approaching the heads from the south; and knowing the number of fatal wrecks that had occurred through Palliser Bay being mistaken for Wellington Harbour, he was very anxious for the thick mist to lift that hung over the land, before running too far in.

When a good sight of the hills was at last obtained, he found in his anxiety to give the fatal bay a wide berth, that he had kept her away too much and had overrun the entrance.

It then became a question whether he should bring the cutter up in the wind, and beat back, or run her through the straits and round Cape Terawiti to Porirua, where there was good anchorage under Mana Island.

The fact of the cutter leaking a good deal when close-hauled, and thereby damaging the cargo, decided him in favour of the latter course, though this he said had its drawback; as the tide being about half ebb and with the southerly wind, and the sea there was, he knew we should have to encounter a frightful tide-rip off Terawiti.

With the wind and sea right aft we were not long in finding his opinion verified.

In the terrific uproar, and commotion of hissing, seething water in which we soon found ourselves, our tiny craft appeared to me no more than a cork in the Norwegian Maelstrom, and we seemed nearly as impotent to control her movements; anon, we were almost buried in the trough of the sea, with an almost perpendicular wall of green water on either side, so much higher than the mast that the mainsail flapped against the topping lifts, and the boom, relieved from all strain, would have been jerked inboard if F. had not taken the precaution some time before, of having a guy attached to it from for'ard; then instead of being swallowed up, as seemed inevitable, the gulf would widen and rolling beneath us would as suddenly elevate us to its crest, when a few brief moments in the gale just sufficed to give the requisite momentum to barely preserve steerage way when becalmed in the trough of the boiling sea.

At last, we had the supreme satisfaction of rounding the cape and gradually edging into smooth water. I felt immensely relieved at what I could not help thinking was a providential escape, but this was my first experience. F. said he had often been caught in it before, only perhaps not so close to the cape as on this occasion.

F. found he could dispose of the cargo to advantage at Porirua and consulted me in reference to it, for selling involved the necessity of returning to Nelson to purchase another.

However much I might regret the delay this would cause, I could not object when there was an opportunity of clearing about £50 by its sale, seeing that he had been subjected to a constant drain the last two months, and nothing had been coming in.

He had nine tons of flour, which was put on board in Nelson at £10 per ton, and about one ton of bacon, costing $4\frac{1}{2}d$. per lb., and the prices offered were £13 10s. for the flour, and $6\frac{1}{2}d$. the bacon, thus netting about £50; it was also essential that the upper works of the cutter should be fresh caulked before going south, as her leaking had been the cause of our running back.

Accordingly, the flour and bacon were landed, and in a couple of days after leaving Porirua we were once more inside the Nelson boulder bank.

While lying at Porirua, I heard of a singular impromptu cruise of one of the small coasters that frequented the place, that fortunately was unattended with any more serious results than a little loss of time.

The vessel arrived at dusk one evening, the anchor was let go, a certain length of chain paid out, and the two men in charge tired out, it may be supposed, with thrashing through the straits against a head wind, immediately turned into their bunks, determined to have a long watch below.

Next morning when the skipper thrust his head out of the small companion hatch to to have a look round, he was quite taken aback, could not comprehend appearances, rubbed his eyes, and was persuaded some wonderful transformation of the land had taken place, and at last he shouted to his mate to tumble on deck as there had been an earthquake in the night, and Mana Island swallowed up.

The mate, after a surprised gaze all round, expressed his opinion that they were in the Sound, and immediately went for'ard to look at the bows, when the mystery was explained. When the anchor was let go the previous night, one of its flukes caught in the bobstay, and while they slept she had drifted harmlessly across the straits, the ebb tide setting her into the northern entrance of the Sound, and when the discovery was made they were just off Ship's Cove.

It was a most providential escape, for she must have drifted in the direction of, and very near to, the reef at Jackson's Head, when the ebb tide caught her and carried her away from the danger into the Sound; otherwise the same current, which here divides, would have swept her past, perhaps foul of the Brothers, two small rocky islands to the south of the entrance.

Shortly after our first start for the South, F. intimated to me the probability of his also settling at Port Cooper if he found remunerative employment for the cutter there, and proposed in that case to join partnership with me in the store business, to which arrangement I was quite agreeable. He was at this time engaged to Miss E., the second eldest daughter of my old friend the shipwright—and confided to me his intention, if everything went on satisfactorily, of returning to Nelson in two or three months and getting married.

Our unexpected return to Nelson so soon, led to an important change in one part of his plans, as far as the lady was concerned, for during our brief stay, while the cutter was being caulked, and a fresh cargo bought and shipped, he got married, and when in a few days a new departure was taken we had a lady passenger, his bride, on board.

We had light and moderately fair winds to the Kaikoras, the noted sticking point on this part of the coast, when as before a stiff sou'-wester set in; but this time there was no running back, the vessel was tight and trim, and if it blew great guns we were determined to ride it out.

When night came and the wind had increased, having plenty of sea-room we lay-to with a balance reefed mainsail, and were quite snug and comfortable, while the wind was piping and whistling through the blocks and rigging, and, though in a very heavy sea, very little water came on board.

Just before dark we observed a schooner about our own size a few miles ahead, apparently bound south; not seeing her next morning we concluded she had turned tail in the night and run back, which we afterwards learnt was the case, as she arrived in Port Cooper about ten days after our coming to an anchorage there.

We held our own pretty well during the three days the gale lasted, rather fore-reaching if anything; then, after a few hours in the doldrums, rolling helplessly on the heavy swell, on the evening of the third day a northerly wind sprang up, and we expected to make the peninsula by daylight next morning.

During the night the wind died away, and at daylight we found that a strong current or the tide had set us close in shore in Pegasus Bay, somewhere near what is now called the New Brighton Beach; the heavy swell was setting us into shallow water, and we had to rig out a couple of long sweeps, and pull our hardest to prevent her being hove ashore.

After about two hours of this work, pulling almost parallel with the beach on account of the swell, but gradually edging her head off shore, we fortunately got into a current that I now know must have been the mouth of the Waimakariri, which soon swept her out to an offing, when sail was hoisted and we stood out in the direction of the end of the peninsula, keenly scanning the shore for any opening, as this was F.'s first visit to this part of New Zealand.

It was not long before Godley Head and the entrance to the harbour opened out; we were soon inside, and observing what appeared to be a number of tents at the bottom of a small bay on our port, the bowline was hauled to windward, and the dingy lowered, and F. sculled ashore to reconnoitre before taking in the cutter.

On his return, he reported that what we supposed were tents, were large piles of whales' bones whitening in the sun.

Down South. 193

This was little Port Cooper, a noted rendezvous for whalers in former times, when whales were very numerous on this part of the coast, and it was here that the whales were towed when captured to be tried out on shore, as being more conveniently and expeditiously managed than on board ship.

Continuing our course up the harbour, it was not until Officers' Point was rounded that any sign of life or settlement appeared, and then a bustling, busy scene was disclosed.

Just as we dropped anchor, I observed a piece of white calico, an apology for a flag, run up to the top of a tall pole; but as there was an immediate cessation of hammering, and work generally, I concluded that this was the 12 o'clock dinner hour signal, and not out of compliment to the distinguished visitors who had just arrived.

After stowing the sails and making things snug on board, F. and I jumped into the dingy and pulled ashore, and at once proceeded to interview Captain Thomas.

We explained our objects and intentions, and he expressed himself as pleased and willing to further them as far as possible. He purchased the flour and chartered the cutter to proceed to Akaloa Bay to load timber for Port, as there was about 100,000 feet ready for conveyance; this promised plenty of work for the cutter.

He also gave us permission to select a site for the store on the part of Norwich Quay or Canterbury Street then formed, explaining that he could give no right of occupation; we should have to arrange with the future owner after the land was selected.

On inspecting the sites indicated I gave my opinion in favour of Canterbury Street, although it involved cutting into a high bank, judging that its future rental would be less than the front street, while it would suit our business quite as well, perhaps better; as being a port town, and Norwich Quay of limited extent, I thought it might be often monopolised by drunken sailors.

During the day a tent was rigged with the cutter's square sail and yard; two or three days sufficed to land everything, and F. started to the bays for the first load of timber, while I began the erection of the house, and as so much

Down South.

of the work had been prepared beforehand, this did not occupy much time.

This was the first shop for the sale of general stores opened in Canterbury; as before we commenced business, provisions, and a few articles in general demand, were only procurable from the proprietors of the Mitre Tavern, who were glad to be relieved of the trouble of keeping such things on sale, their licensed business at this time demanding all their attention.

For some time after commencing business, great inconvenience was occasioned by the almost total absence of small change; those old-fashioned round wooden boxes of matches, which are seldom seen now, and sticks of tobacco, each valued at 3*d.*, were the chief medium of exchange; as the liberal proprietors of the only licensed house charged the same for a glass of ale for which it is now sold, namely, 3*d.*, it was easy to detect a thirsty votary of Bacchus, whose libations were not deep, but frequent, from the distension of his pockets by the aforesaid bulky boxes of lucifers, one being given as a matter of course, as change upon the consumption of each glass of beer. Sometimes I would receive a visit from one of these itinerant match depôts, wishing to be relieved of his stock at half price.

I soon found there would be a good sale for bread if a baker's business were started, and saw no great difficulty in supplying the want —given the oven and flour, I did not doubt that the loaves would follow.

In the high solid bank at the rear of the store, I considered was a capital site for an oven; this I dug out the requisite size, leaving a bench of the proper height for the sole or bottom of the oven, and when excavated I was forcibly reminded of the wharé at Wakapuaka, of which it was almost a facsimile on a small scale.

From a gully opposite I carried as many stones as sufficed for the bottom and sides, and facing the front with a wall, and from having the solid bank on either side and the back, no iron work was needed for ties, etc.

I then applied to Captain Thomas for a few hundred of bricks for the crown and chimney,

Down South. 197

which he very kindly spared to me for such a purpose.

As I was quite ignorant of the process of making bread on a large scale, I made inquiries among the workmen, and at last found a youth who had formerly been employed to carry out bread for a Wellington baker, and had also occasionally assisted in the bakehouse.

He was at once engaged, some dried yeast procured from Wellington, and the dough for the first batch of loaves made for sale in Canterbury was mixed in a large washing-tub, and turned out quite a success.

In a short time I made a suitable trough, and provided other conveniences for carrying on the business, which proved a valuable auxiliary to the general store, and was of great convenience to the public, as very few of the workmen were married men, or if married, had their wives with them at Lyttelton at this time. Lyttelton has always been badly supplied with fresh water; at this time there was only one well, and it had been sunk in the vicinity of the immigration barracks then in course of erection on the east side of Oxford

Street; but down on the beach at the bottom of a high bank, opposite the Mitre, there was a little trickle of fresh water, that accumulating in a hollow, afforded a limited supply to those in its immediate neighbourhood.

In order to monopolise this supply as far as possible, an old man (who gained a living by making and selling ginger beer) had built his wharé on the top of the bank, directly above it, and it required the utmost caution to forestall him in the early morning.

Just at daybreak I used to creep softly down with a couple of buckets, fearful of making the slightest noise, as being so near he could so quickly empty the hollow, and then it would take some time to again collect a fresh supply, and there was also the chance of the tide spoiling it and causing further delay.

CHAPTER IX.

A STEP UPWARD.

CAPTAIN THOMAS, who had been deputed to select a block of land suitable for the projected "Church of England Settlement," had chosen the Port Cooper plains, and decided upon the present site of Lyttelton as the most eligible for a port town. At the time of my arrival, in December, 1849, he had about one hundred Maories (brought from the North Island), and from sixty to seventy Europeans (carpenters, labourers, and navvies), actively employed in and about the port erecting barracks, road making, and otherwise endeavouring to improve the aspect of the naturally rugged and unprepossessing appearance of the site chosen. Several parties of surveyors were at the same time engaged in making a trigonometrical survey of the plains, and mapping out the future city of Christchurch and its suburbs.

As we at once began to do a fair amount of business, it was a subject of surprise to me that this field of enterprise, in a small way, had remained unoccupied so long, considering that Wellington was so near, and small craft dropping in at short intervals; and notwithstanding the various misfortunes that had delayed our arrival for about two months, it was reserved for us to have the honour and emolument of first breaking ground in this important and flourishing province.

I have characterised my occupation on the roads, socially considered, as a "step downward"; I feel that I am quite justified by the result of subsequent experience in regarding this as so important a point in my career as to merit the designation of a "step upward."

Some time in April, 1850, Mr. Godley arrived in the 'Lady Nugent'; his fiat went forth, and this busy scene of industry was suddenly changed. His mission was to stop all expenditure until further orders, as at the time of his leaving England serious doubts

A Step Upward.

were entertained of the Canterbury Association being able to launch their scheme with any great probability of success.

Mr. Godley re-embarked in the 'Lady Nugent,' and continued his voyage to Wellington to wait the course of events in England. Immediately after his departure arrangements were made for re-conveying to Wellington those Maories who desired to return, according to stipulations made at the time of their engagement; and nearly all availed themselves of the opportunity.

Captain Thomas was very much disconcerted at his labours being brought to such a sudden standstill, particularly as he had just commenced cutting through a high bank in order to form a roadway connecting Oxford and Canterbury Streets, now known as Norwich Quay. Having a strong desire to complete this work, he made arrangements for carrying out his object, that would be considered unique at the present time.

He assembled the men, told them his position and wishes, stating that he had neither cash nor credit available for continuing the work, but that there was a large stock of nails, paint, tar, linseed oil, tools, and lumber of various kinds, which he was prepared to deal out in lieu of cash payments for wages, and he hoped they would stick to the work until the cutting was carried through, as he was confident the settlement would go on, and this was a work most essential for traffic, as well as adding greatly to the appearance of the place.

The men cheerfully fell in with his views, stuck to the work, and carried it through to completion. How the men managed to digest the nails, and eke out a precarious existence upon coal tar, and paint oil, deponent sayeth not. The business, which had so far been very flourishing, fell to a very low ebb after the departure of the Maories, and many of the other workers, after the total withdrawal of the wages fund hitherto expended.

The cutter was still employed in the conveyance of timber from the bays, with an occasional trip to Sumner; but at about the time of the stoppage of the works F. was laid up with a severe cold and slight fever, and another had taken his place in the cutter for

A Step Upward. 203

a few trips. One evening at this time it came on to blow a gale from the south-west; in the afternoon the cutter had returned from Sumner in ballast, after discharging which she went along the Oxford Street jetty (then in course of construction) to take in another load for Sumner in the morning. The person in charge of the cutter was at the house that evening reading a book when it began to blow, and immediately left to get the cutter away from the jetty, out to a safe anchorage. Shortly afterwards, as the wind increased very much, I walked down to the jetty, as I was anxious to know if the cutter had been moored a safe distance from it, and was very much concerned at finding they had only been able to get a very short distance from the jetty, and from where she was anchored with the dingy astern, the latter was only a few yards from the piles and scaffolding of the unfinished wharf. The gale had come on with such sudden violence that they had not been able to get far enough to give her the benefit of a good length of cable.

While waiting and watching, and fearing she could not hold out long, I was surprised and grieved to find F., whom I had left ill in bed, by my side. Hearing the terrific rush of the wind, and fearing the worst by my not returning, he had, in defiance of the entreaties of his wife, come down to know how matters stood. He immediately told those on board to cast loose the dingy, so as to give the cutter all the chain the short distance would allow. This was done, and the dingy was crushed up like a match-box in a few seconds. By some unfortunate mischance in easing the cable it was let run off the belaying bits, and in an instant almost the cutter was smashing among the piles and cross-timbers of the unfinished jetty. The cutter was a complete wreck, and was sold a day or two afterwards to the contractors who were building the jetty for £25.

But this was a trifling matter compared to its effect upon F.; his leaving a sick bed and being exposed to such inclement weather, together with anxiety from the loss of the cutter, quite prostrated him, an accession of fever supervened, and in three weeks after this stormy night he left a young widow to mourn his loss. He died the 13th of May, 1850, and after the funeral Mrs. F. resided for a short time with a family settled in port—old Nelson

A Step Upward. 205

acquaintances—until there was a vessel sailing for either Nelson or Wellington, in one of which she took passage, being anxious to rejoin her mother and sister in Nelson.

After this brief enjoyment of the advantages and comforts of a settled home, and sanguine anticipations of our mutually achieving a large measure of success in our new venture in the course of a few years, this was a crushing blow that broke up a cheerful and happy home, and committed me once again to a lonely isolation.

Some time before this I had been obliged to dismiss the lad on account of his becoming too impudent and independent, thinking himself indispensable in the baking business. But this I was very soon competent to manage without his assistance, though I would gladly have kept him had he behaved properly. I had been in the habit of assisting him and waiting upon him almost like a boy, until he presumed too much, and I was obliged to dismiss him. One morning shortly before this he said he would show me a little experiment, that might have resulted in very serious consequences to himself. The dough had been made and was proving, and the wood was in full blaze in the oven, when with a pair of bellows he puffed away until all the flame was extinguished, and then he threw in a match. I was standing on one side of the oven opening, wondering what result was to follow; as there was no immediate effect he advanced to look in, when a large volume of flame issued from the oven mouth, singeing the whiskers off one side of my face, and causing him to fall back shrieking with agony. I immediately laid him on his back and grated a quantity of raw potato upon his face. This was not only comforting from its coolness, giving immediate relief from pain, but had a remarkably healing effect, as in about a week his face was quite well, only the loss of his eyebrows and front hair gave him rather a comical aspect.

From the diminished demand for bread after the departure of so many of the workmen, I did not find it necessary to bake oftener than once or twice a week; and being alone, with the shop to attend to, I used to set the sponge, so as to bake in the evening after the shop was closed; a batch of eighty or a hundred loaves,

A Step Upward. 207

and attending to the oven, keeping me actively engaged from eight till twelve, by which time I generally had it all set in the oven, and by the time it was drawn it was generally between one and two before my work was all done and I retired to rest. One baking night, thinking I should like something tasty for supper, and taking mental stock of the few available comestibles, I decided in favour of an apple-pie, which, according to my benighted notions, I thought could be quickly prepared and baked with the bread. I therefore filled a pie dish with American dried apples from a cask in the store, added some water, and flattened out one of the unbaked loaves for a crust, which I duly placed over the apples, and as it was for my sole delectation I dispensed with all but adventitious ornamentation. When the batch was all in, the pie was placed in front near the entrance. At the appointed time for drawing the loaves the oven was opened, when, lo! the phenomenon that presented itself! I dimly recognized the dish from its outline remaining unchanged, but in other respects the pie was a fearful and mysterious looking object.

I had sufficient judgment left (which from the foregoing might perhaps be doubted) to discover the rationale of the strange apparition. The apples had plimmed, as it is called, with the water added, and lifted the crust from the dish, thereby losing their protection from the fierce heat, and presented a black stratum like a thin seam of coal; the crust asserting its prerogative of bread dough, had also mounted upwards in a pyramidal form, reaching nearly to the crown of the oven. I need not add that my supper was a failure.

After the works were stopped, and Captain Thomas made his novel arrangement for their partial resumption, as might have been expected, some few did not accept the terms, but preferred to loaf about the beach and public-house, and it became a serious consideration for those who had anything to lose to devise protective measures. As there was but one policeman, no one dreamt of his services being available if required; it used to be a mystery to me how he managed to relieve guard. Occupying a house alone, and having many things likely to be "*wanted*," I was apprehensive every night of receiving a visit from some of these gentry, and from sheer politeness was chiefly anxious not to be caught "napping." It was my custom every night to pile a lot of pannikins and other tin ware, etc., at the weak places of my citadel, where a breach was most likely to be made, so that a tremendous clatter would be the result of even a slight disturbance of their arrangement. I had also provided myself with a bayonet securely fixed on a stout staff about four feet long; this I was advised was a better weapon than a pistol, as not being liable to miss fire.

Whether my precautions became known, and a warm reception anticipated, or not, I do not know; my place remained unmolested until urgent business connected with my late partnership obliged me to go to Wellington and leave my place in charge of another, when shortly after my departure an entrance was effected, and a considerable booty carried off. Fortunately the greater part was recovered a few days after the robbery by the accidental discovery of the place where it had been planted round Officers' Point, conveniently for conveying away by boat.

Just before the suspension of the works, some amusingly descriptive lines appeared in one of the Wellington or Nelson papers upon 'Vancouver's Island,' and being very characteristic of the state of things in Lyttelton at that time, they had a great charm for Captain Thomas, and tickled his fancy immensely. While superintending the erection of the *palatial* future residence of the expected agent of the Canterbury Association (now used as offices of the Borough Council) he was frequently heard singing, to an improvised tune,

> The Governor's dwelling, all others excelling;
> A door and two windows in front!
> In front!
> A door and two windows in front!

Our chief functionary at this time was H. G. Gouland, Esq., Collector of Customs, Resident Magistrate, Deputy Registrar, Police Inspector, etc., etc.; indeed, combining in his own person all the dignity and authority of the British Constitution. As an official he was fussy, methodical, and a red-tapeist; but out of office personal acquaintances found him

A Step Upward.

a genial and pleasant gentleman, possessed of a large fund of valuable information and experience.

A trifling incident in connection with his first arrival in this settlement may be considered characteristic. The vessel that he took passage in at Wellington for Lyttelton struck a rock near the Wellington Heads, and it was thought by those on board that she would founder. Our future dignitary was calmly reposing in a berth below, and heard the frantic rushing to and fro, and the noise and apparent confusion that prevailed on deck, but did not stir. After a brief interval a seaman rushed below and advised him to hasten on deck, as the vessel was sinking and the crew getting out the boats. He quietly said, "For God's sake let me go to the bottom in my berth instead of going on deck and getting my legs broken first." It was afterwards found the damage was not so extensive as at first supposed; the vessel continued her course, the serenity of Her Majesty's representative remained undisturbed, and he eventually arrived safe at his destination.

Some time during the year 1850, while the aforesaid gentleman was "administering the Government," a schooner that usually traded between the settlements (provinces were unknown at that date) dropped anchor one morning, and the skipper, deeming he was beyond the pale of all Customs' restrictions, made no secret of his having some genuine "mountain dew" on board, that he had not considered it necessary to go through the formality of inserting in the Manifest, and of which he was prepared to give his customers the benefit.

Our C. C. quickly hired a boat, for, be it observed, he was also his own landing waiter, and boarded the schooner while the said skipper was entertaining his friends at the Mitre, but not finding anything "contraband" returned in disgust, thinking he had been hoaxed. The captain was soon heard boasting that the "old fool" had sat on the casks in the cabin without knowing it. Not to be beaten, a second, and this time not unsuccessful, visit was paid to the vessel, and the "illicit" duly brought on shore. The loquacious skipper lost no time in getting on board, tripping his anchor, and

A Step Upward. 213

putting to sea, with less " spirits " than when he arrived, but pleased withal at having saved his vessel.

There was also residing in Lyttelton a genial, unostentatious gentleman, who must have been blissfully unconscious at this time of the multitudinous offices and honours in store for him by a Government not remarkable for making the happiest selections of its subordinates. But in his case the numerous and varied offices were filled with such fidelity, exactitude, ability, and tact, as won golden opinions from every one. And he continues to command the respect, almost veneration, of the entire community for his many sterling qualities, and the long and valuable services he has rendered to the public from the very foundation of the settlement to the present day. May he long continue to wear and enjoy his well-merited honours!

I cannot help noticing that about this time there was a very general impression among the beachites that the Canterbury Association scheme must collapse, and the settlement be abandoned. I did not share this feeling; I felt convinced that however circumstances might necessitate a modification of the original plans it was morally certain that a settlement of some kind would be formed, considering the fine extent of suitable country that abounded in this locality. And with this faith, as my time was not fully occupied, I procured timber and doubled the original size of my store, thereby exciting the wonder and almost pity of some of my neighbours, who could not understand such infatuation.

After the 'Lady Nugent,' the 'Mariner' was the next ship arriving direct from England, and although she brought no certain intelligence of the doings of the Canterbury Association, I learnt that there were certain stores on board sent out by the Association for the use of the settlement, and consigned to Captain Thomas, which I considered as indirectly indicating that there was no present intention of abandoning the enterprise. The captain brought his ship to an anchor just inside Godley Head, and was pulled ashore in his gig, being desirous of landing his freight with as little delay as possible, and proceeding on his voyage.

After a brief interview with the Collector of Customs, and finding that he would not be allowed to land anything unless he regularly entered his vessel, he declared his intention of carrying the goods to Wellington, to which port his ship was consigned, rather than submit to the delay of entering her at the Customs; and accordingly hastened down to his boat at the jetty, and returned to his ship.

As the arrival of an English ship was quite an event at this time, I gladly accepted the offer of a seat in a neighbour's boat, who was going off to the vessel. While on board I was pleased to find among her passengers an uncle and aunt of F., my late partner, who were going to Nelson to settle. As the gentleman expressed a great desire to land to see the township, and a fellow-passenger also wished to accompany him, we took them on shore. They had not been long on shore when they observed the captain's boat pushing off from the jetty. As the captain before going on shore had issued orders that no one was to leave the ship during his absence, they hurried down to the beach, engaged a waterman's boat, and followed in his wake. The captain, recognizing the occupants of the boat, ordered his men to "give way," and the light boat, impelled by four strong rowers, soon left the passengers hopelessly in the rear. The boatman was urged to put on all steam, and was also stimulated to increased exertions by promises of liberal payment; but with an easterly wind and a lumpy sea their progress was necessarily slow, and they had the mortification of seeing the captain's boat reach the ship, and immediately afterwards slung to the davits, the anchor tripped, and the vessel with spreading sails standing out to sea. The boatman wished to give up the apparently hopeless chase, but renewed offers of reward induced him to continue the struggle, and they were on the point of abandoning the pursuit, when, observing the topsail aback, they knew the captain had relented, and was waiting for them.

After this lesson, and on regaining the ship a sharp lecture for disobeying orders, they rejoined their late sorrowing friends, who had almost begun to regard them as a couple of involuntary Robinson Crusoes.

A Step Upward. 217

The next arrival from England was the 'Phœbe Dunbar,' bringing certain intelligence of the sailing of the first four ships with Canterbury settlers, which put us all on the *qui vive*. When the news reached Wellington Mr. Godley hastened down, and I have no doubt was much pleased at the improvements Captain Thomas had effected on Norwich Quay during his absence, under the new Public Works Policy he had initiated. A party of men were at once set to work on the Sumner Road, under the desperate pretence of opening out that line for the transit of the settlers and their luggage to the plains; but as there were some doubts of this being accomplished in time, another party of men were employed in forming a shorter cut over the hills, since known as the "bridle path."

The prospect of such an influx of settlers had a powerful attraction for all the loose elements of Wellington. Small craft were continually arriving, each with its quota of passengers, actuated by the most philanthropic solicitude to minister to the wants of the expected immigrants.

Monday morning, December 16th, 1850, a glorious New Zealand summer morning, fit to usher in a week fraught with such important consequences to this port, and indeed the whole of New Zealand. About 10 A.M. a large ship (the 'Charlotte Jane') suddenly appeared round Officers' Point (she had not been observed coming up the harbour), and brought to an anchor opposite the town, where only small coasters afterwards deemed it prudent to lie. We had not even a " Harbour Master in charge of a punt " at that time, and being previous to the engineering works of the " hard labour gang," probably there was a greater depth of water in that part of the harbour than at the present time. The 'Randolph' arrived about 3 P.M. the same day, and the 'Sir George Seymour' at 10 A.M. on the 17th, the 'Cressy' not putting in an appearance until the 27th.

Great was the excitement and commotion in our small township from such an influx of strangers. The commissariat resources of the place became at once an important consideration, seeing that besides my own there were but two or three small stores that had recently sprung up. Mine was also the only baker's shop; fortunately I had secured the services of a journeyman bread-baker from Wellington; the capabilities of the oven were taxed to the utmost, and could then only supply about one tithe of the demand. A hungry crowd collected morning and evening round the door about the time of drawing the batch, and the loaves were quickly distributed to the fortunate few nearest at hand. This scramble for bread was a daily scene in Canterbury Street for a fortnight, until other ovens were built, when supply and demand became somewhat equalised.

It was with feelings of no little surprise and dismay that the new arrivals, on preparing to land the various etceteras that provident and well-to-do colonists considered indispensable in a new and comparatively unknown country, found themselves confronted by a Custom House officer. However pleasing it may have been as a matter of sentiment to feel the protecting solicitude of Her Most Gracious Majesty extended to this distant part of her dominions, the predominant feeling just then was that it was not alone a trifle inconvenient, but extremely vexatious. Fortunately a deliverer was at hand. Sir G. Grey had arrived in H. M. S. 'Fly' the same day as the 'Charlotte Jane,' and upon being appealed to he at once graciously removed the restrictions that an otherwise too rigid adherence to red-tapeism would have imposed upon the first arrivals.

A printing press, type, and a printing staff had arrived by one of the first ships, and by unremitting exertions on the part of all interested the public had the advantage and great gratification of very early welcoming the appearance of the first newspaper published in the settlement. The first number of the 'Lyttelton Times' was issued on Saturday, January 11th, 1851, four weeks previous to which press, type, printers, and settlers had not arrived on the coast of New Zealand. More than a quarter of a century has elapsed since that date, during which the settlement, like all young communities, has passed through various vicissitudes, — periods of alternate prosperity and depression. But there has been no retrogression. It has ever been pressing onward, and the newspaper has

A Step Upward.

kept on the even tenour of its way, a true index of the progress made, and marking the successive stages of provincial development, by passing from a weekly to a bi-weekly, tri-weekly, and eventually to a morning and evening issue, and now supports two morning and two evening papers.

About this time my former companion in the Wellington store, who so signally failed in initiating me into the noble art of "self-defence," being unemployed, came down on a Micawberlike speculation of something turning up, and was not disappointed; for being in want of help, and knowing his value in a store like mine, I was glad of the chance of securing his services. He remained with me for about two years, when he succeeded to a business in Wellington; this was afterwards relinquished in favour of an important post under the Provincial Government at Wellington, which he still holds. Some time ago he was referred to in one of the Wellington papers as the most efficient and valuable officer of the Provincial Government.

For about six weeks after the arrival of the first ships the weather continued remarkably fine, deluding the settlers into the belief that we almost enjoyed a tropical climate. This continuance of fine weather was of great advantage, as besides the paucity of house accommodation, the conveniencies for landing cargo were very limited, much of it having to be done by ships' boats, and landing on the beach in front of Norwich Quay as often as at the one small jetty. Two or three watermen's boats brought down from Wellington by their enterprising owners found lucrative employment in towing through the sea hogsheads of brandy, etc., from the ship's side to the same landing-place.

All persons occupying the barracks had, after a brief sojourn there, to give place to others, and the hill-side, near the barracks, became dotted over with every conceivable kind of hut, tent, and wharé, not omitting the Irish cabin built of sods. Some whose constructive abilities were exemplified by tenements of the rudest character and materials of the flimsiest description, were cautioned that a sou'-wester might spring up very suddenly, accompanied with heavy rain, against which their dwellings

A Step Upward. 223

would afford them no protection; but conviction and procrastination often go hand in hand.

The weather changed very suddenly; a boisterous sou'-wester, known as a "southerly buster," with a deluge of rain, caused a rude awakening of the poor "pilgrims" encamped on the hill-side. Tents were seen in every stage of collapse; blankets, toi-toi, and fern careering madly through the air, and the houseless seeking and finding shelter wherever a good Samaritan could take them in.

A local artist of a humorous turn executed a spirited sketch of these fugitive tenements while undergoing the process of disintegration, the fidelity of which, and elaboration of the details supplied, caused his friends to believe he must have executed it while taking shelter from the storm under the great bell of St. Michael's, at that time temporarily set up on the bank.

Curiosity and a desire for trade, the latter perhaps being the stronger motive, had attracted large numbers of Maories from the adjacent bays and the Peninsula, so that the settlers had an early introduction to the Queen's aboriginal subjects. The inevitable war-dance was performed to a numerous, if not appreciative, audience. A motley and partially nude mob mustered at the junction of Oxford and London Streets armed with sticks and the leg-bones of cattle, in lieu of ordinary native weapons, when one of their number advanced to the front and was supposed to be delivering a very exciting address, extolling the deeds of some noted chief of their party or tribe, commending their own invincible courage, the weakness of the enemy, and the promise of an easy victory, and cannibal feast to follow; and during its recital he walked rapidly to and fro in front of them, delivering himself in an excited, jerky, spasmodic manner; then, with hideous grimaces, a rush was made by the whole body of them along London Street, and at its junction with Canterbury Street a halt was made, and another warlike orator advanced to the front, and a repetition of the proceedings followed.

After the foregoing a liberal supply of flour and sugar (ordered, it was understood, by Sir G. Grey) was distributed among the sable warriors. As they nearly all wore at that time the ordinary native costume, a dirty sort of whitey-brown blanket, no difficulty was found in disposing of the rations of flour and sugar, one corner of the blanket being appropriated to the flour and another to the sugar. One individual, called the " market gardener," whose success in the vegetable line had enabled him to don a blue frock coat, black cloth trousers, Wellington boots, and a tall hat, found himself at a disadvantage as compared with his brethren in having no convenient receptacle for his share of the flour and sugar. He surveyed his hat, but replaced it on his head, evidently considering it unequal to the emergency, unless he chose to sacrifice a portion of the allotted quantity, when a happy thought struck him. To the intense amusement of the bystanders he took off his Wellington boots; but this was not accomplished without a great deal of frantic pulling and hauling, having just gone through the violent athletic exercise of the war-dance in them, and carried off in triumph his share of the flour in one and sugar in the other.

Immigrants arriving in Canterbury at the

present time, provided with an easy and rapid transit to comfortable and roomy barracks, a bountiful supply of good wholesome food, and surrounded by all the conveniences of civilization, can have little or no conception of the trials and difficulties experienced by the first settlers at the time of which I am writing, whether as regards house accommodation or getting themselves and their chattels transported to Christchurch and the plains. And these trials were shared alike by gentle and simple, employer and employé, land purchaser and labourer.

I remember a lady, now living in Christchurch, saying to me in a laughing manner a few days before leaving Lyttelton for the plains, that she was very glad at the prospect of a little more freedom, as she had found it very irksome living with her pots and kettles, alluding to the one room at the barracks, about ten by twelve, occupied by herself, husband, and daughter, and which had to do duty as bed-room, sitting-room, and kitchen.

Others with large families were even more sorely inconvenienced. The genial good humour

A Step Upward.

with which all these little trials were encountered and overcome was quite refreshing to witness; and then the sums that had to be paid for the conveyance of luggage and all personal effects in boats by way of Sumner to Christchurch, and the tramp over the range to Christchurch by ladies unaccustomed to much walking, are matters still held in remembrance, I have no doubt, by the fair pedestrians. In addition to the great expense incurred in sending goods by the boats, there was also the uncertainty of when they would reach their destination, as the Sumner bar sometimes caused considerable delay. For one or both of these reasons it was customary for parties migrating to the plains to load themselves with everything portable, and that could not even temporarily be dispensed with.

One evening, about a month after the arrival of the first ships, I was returning to port, having visited with a friend the Messrs. Deans, at Riccarton, and had just waded through the swamp that lay in the line of march, which could not be avoided, when I met a middle-aged man carrying a towering bundle, which I concluded to be a bed. A few chains in the rear was his wife, also carrying a bundle nearly as large as the one carried by her husband. Shortly after I encountered the eldest son, who was staggering under a heavy load. Then appeared one of the daughters, and finally I passed two more sons, a daughter, and one or two little ones all more or less loaded. They had walked with their loads from Port, and it was their intention to camp near the site of the house that had yet to be built.

I merely give this as one instance, but it was of daily occurrence the first few months of 1851. The person here referred to is now living in the suburbs of Christchurch, having retired from business. I frequently meet him now, but under what changed circumstances! He is generally accompanied in his carriage by his wife and some members of his family; the sons are thriving in various businesses in the city, and he is, I hope, in the full enjoyment of a well-earned repose, after the heat of the day, cherishing, I have no doubt, a kindly remembrance of the early trials and difficulties of founding a new home in a strange land, which a few years of persevering effort successfully accomplished.

In addition to the stream of pedestrians, loaded with every conceivable article pertaining to household and culinary use, to be met wending their weary way from the Port to the embryo city and various parts of the plains, resembling more the hasty retreat from a hotly-besieged town than the exodus of a determined band of pilgrims bent upon establishing homes in this land of promise, were also to be seen certain enterprising Christchurch storekeepers, who were under the necessity of making frequent trips to and from Port for such goods as were in request, and which could not wait the tardy transit by boat, and who, in the interest of their customers and the exigencies of trade, did not hesitate to transform themselves into pack-horses for the nonce, and carry loads of such a size and weight that made the new arrivals just off a long sea voyage marvel at their muscular powers and staying qualities, for, as I observed, these herculean feats were frequently undertaken two or three times a week. It is pleasing to be able to record that a well-merited success in trade attended such persevering efforts, and that some of them are still among us, quietly reposing upon the results of their exertions.

The advent of the "Bishop Designate!" With what feelings of exultation his arrival was hailed! what exalted expectations were entertained of the benefits that were to flow from the founding, the consolidating, and crowning of the Episcopal edifice of the youngest section of the English Church in this the youngest of the English settlements, and that were to result from the residence and guidance of a Bishop! There was a great blowing of trumpets over this affair, but, alas! his stay was of the briefest, and serious was the disappointment his hasty departure caused. The title long lingered in the minds of the inhabitants.

I remember when Sir William Congreve was a candidate for a newly-created office under one of the ordinances of the first Provincial Council he used to be referred to as the "Scab-Inspector Designate." This meteoric visit was regarded by many as a great "sham," not that anything unworthy was imputed to the high-minded gentlemen associated together for the purpose of founding a Church of England settlement in New Zealand, and who in their zeal for transporting a section of the Church, complete in all its parts, considered it of paramount importance that the flock should be presided over by a Bishop.

Nevertheless, a strong opinion prevailed that his brief visit was only intended to give *éclat* to the enterprise, and to attract land purchasers, which received strong confirmation when it became known that from the land sales having fallen very far short of the reasonable expectations of the founders of the settlement, the latter not only individually advanced large sums, but the financial necessities of the Association had obliged the borrowing of the £10,000 allocated to the "Bishopric Endowment Fund," so that, until this was restored to its original uses, it was vain to hope for the consecration of a Bishop to the see. The visit of the Bishop Designate was considered to have utterly failed in its object, and added considerably to the "little bill" of the Canterbury Association against the province, which was ultimately paid from the proceeds of the sale of the town reserves, and thereby deprived the municipality of a future valuable endowment.

I have always thought it a fortunate circumstance that the location of the Canterbury settlers took place at the particular time it did, for had it been delayed twelve months it is certain it would have been wanting in one at least of its chief elements of success, that first assured, and to the present time materially assisted in maintaining its prosperity. I refer to the presence and example of the Australian stockowners and sheep-farmers who arrived in Canterbury almost simultaneously with the English settlers.

The discovery of gold in Australia, which occurred so soon after the formation of this settlement, would have given a different direction to the enterprise and energy of those gentlemen, and the probability is that they would not have been found seeking new country and fresh outlets for their surplus stock in New Zealand, which a knowledge of the projected

A Step Upward. 233

new settlement and its extent of level land had stimulated, station property and stock farming in Australia at that time having almost ceased to be profitable.

To give an idea of the depreciation in value of station property at that time in Australia it is only necessary to refer to accounts of sales that occasionally appeared in the newspapers of that period, showing that stations, with all the sheep depasturing thereon, were frequently sold at a price computed according to the number of sheep, valuing the latter at from fourpence to sixpence per head; and this aggregate sum included station buildings, boiling-down establishments, and all the appurtenances of a first-class station.

These pioneers in New Zealand of the Australian squatters, finding the Canterbury plains eminently adapted for stock-grazing, and the climate of New Zealand promising an immunity from those periodic visitations of floods and droughts, which were frequently so destructive to stock in Australia, may be supposed to have summed up the prospective advantages somewhat in this wise—New and fertile pastures, more lambs, more wool, fewer casualties, and for some, perhaps many years, a good market for stock, dispensing with the boiling-down process. Favourable reports soon found their way into the Port Phillip (Victoria) papers, particularly one written by Mr. Joseph Hawdon, a gentleman upon whose judgment and experience the greatest confidence was placed, and in consequence many others joined in the movement, and a brisk carrying trade of sheep, cattle, and horses to Canterbury was the result.

The Canterbury settlers were not slow in profiting by so good an example, and by entering heartily into the same pursuit very soon convinced their exemplars that they were not deserving of the openly-expressed pity, closely allied to contempt, with which their Australian visitors were disposed to regard them.

In the "Dream of a Shagroon," which bore the date Ko Motinau, April, 1851, and which first appeared in the 'Wellington Spectator' of May 7, the term "Pilgrim" was first applied to the settlers; it was also predicted in it that the "Pilgrims" would be "smashed," and the

A Step Upward. 235

"Shagroons" left in undisputed possession of the country for their flocks and herds. Happily for the mutual advantage of both "Shagroons" and "Pilgrims" the predictions of the former were not verified. It would be a mistake to suppose that in those early days of persistent hard work and dogged endurance there were no softening influences to take off and tone down the rugged asperities of colonial life. Balls, glee-parties, and other social amenities were not wanting as means of relaxation. The impromptu devices and artistic management of incongruous combinations, and amusing makeshifts to achieve a certain result, were not the least pleasing feature of these social reunions, and seemed to give their partakers a keener sense of enjoyment.

The number of pianos imported by the first settlers formed the subject of some depreciatory remarks by one of the Australians in writing to a friend, and, perhaps, unconsciously helped to form the opinion that the "Pilgrims" would never succeed as colonists. On the other hand, it was charitably concluded by the "Pilgrims" that a long deprivation of the refinements of good society had warped the judgment of the "Colonials," causing them to take too cynical a view of the new aids to colonization.

Canterbury used to be regarded by the other provinces as a very aristocratic settlement, and there were very good reasons for this opinion. The principle and object of its foundation had peculiar attractions for a very superior class of settlers not usually found emigrating to the colonies; and bringing with them the refinements, and also a good deal of the exclusiveness, of good society, very sensibly gave a tone and character to the settlement that, notwithstanding the levelling-down tendency of colonial life, it has preserved and maintained to the present day.

In the early days of the settlement instances of this exclusiveness were more frequent and obtrusive than pleasant, and perhaps in resentment for slights of another kind, to none was it more frequently displayed than to the old "Colonials." I remember upon one occasion of a public ball taking place, public so far that the tickets were open for general sale, and upon a certain gentleman (who is now a

A Step Upward. 237

member of the Legislative Council) and his wife presenting their tickets at the door they were refused admission by the doorkeeper, one of the self-elected *élite* who was acting steward for the occasion. The reasons assigned, we may suppose, were so unsatisfactory that our incipient legislator did not pause to argue the point, but forthwith applied a manual tourniquet to another point, to wit, the aforesaid steward's nose, and gave it such a vigorous wrench that, for relief to his lacerated feelings and organ, he applied to that redresser of grievances the R. M. A fine of five pounds was imposed for this *mild* indulgence. The money was paid with cheerful alacrity, the operator remarking that he should be extremely gratified to purchase more of the amusement at the same moderate charge.

CHAPTER X.

A STEP MATRIMONIAL.

It is not given to many men to possess both the commanding talents of Mr. Godley and such an opportunity of exercising them as fell to his lot when he assumed the charge, I may say government, of this Canterbury settlement. In the exercise of his multifarious duties he won the unbounded confidence and esteem of the entire community over which he presided. Whether as champion of the Constitutionalists, who were fighting the battle of freedom, and vainly trying to extort some measure of local self-government from Sir G. Grey, or by an ever-vigilant watchfulness in smoothing difficulties incidental to the first planting of a settlement by modifying and correcting the crude theories and cut-and-dried regulations

A Step Matrimonial. 239

of a distant and almost irresponsible power, ignorant and inexperienced in the varying changes and necessities of a young settlement, his powerful, and at the same time, persuasive and winning eloquence, and his tact and skill as an administrator, were equally conspicuous.

As one illustration out of many of the wonderful power he could wield over an auditory by his suavity and agreeable style and manner, I may instance the first public symptom of dissatisfaction culminating in a kind of indignation meeting being held in Lyttelton by a considerable body of influential land purchasers, whose grievances were that the churches and schools had not been provided by the Association, for which one-third of the price of all the land sold had been allocated. Mixing freely among those present I readily gathered that the prevailing sentiment was strongly condemnatory of the Association, and that it would probably find expression in the passing of some severe resolutions.

This was an opportunity Mr. Godley, as Agent of the Association, could not allow to pass unheeded; indeed, as the sequel showed, he resolved to "improve the occasion." I cannot attempt to indicate his line of argument; he did not betray the slightest feeling of impatience or annoyance at these demands being urged at that particular time, which he might have done, knowing the peculiar financial difficulties with which the Association was then contending, and that Lord Lyttelton and others were then paying large sums from their private purses to meet the heavy preliminary expenses incurred in preparing and founding the settlement.

He delivered a long and eloquent peroration upon the dignity of *work* and the inestimable privilege they each and all shared in assisting to found and build up the institutions of a State and Church in this distant part of the globe, and ended a powerful appeal by proposing to head a subscription list on behalf of the Association with the sum of £500, and a contribution on his own account of £100 towards a fund for the erection of the first church in Canterbury. I need not add that all present warmly responded, and those who came to censure remained to pay.

A Step Matrimonial. 241

A few days after, the subscription list was published amounting to nearly £900. It grieves me to report, that the money raised by so much effort was utterly wasted through the incompetence of either architect or builder, or both, I cannot say which, but the fact remains that it was so faulty in design and construction, and so dangerous when a strong wind was blowing, that it remained unused for two or three years, and when fresh funds were obtained, it was taken down and the present one erected. During the time of its disuse a severe hail-storm broke all the windows facing the harbour, and the building having been condemned, it was unnecessary to expend money in repairs, consequently it remained for about two years a conspicuous and dilapidated-looking object, conveying the impression to strangers that it had sustained a severe siege.

My business continued to prosper, and with the feeling that it was firmly established, came another irrepressible feeling, impelling me to pay a visit to Nelson. An opportunity offering of a small cutter going there direct,

R

I took passage in her, and after a splendid run of forty hours, found myself walking along the old familiar beach-road once more. It is unnecessary to go into the details of this visit; it sufficeth to state that the crowning point of recent successes was achieved by my late partner's eldest sister consenting to become my wife.

It would only be a commonplace truism to state, that the prospect of this to me auspicious event had sustained and stimulated my latter exertions.

It was a proud moment when I, that had been once so cast down, was accepted by one I had long learned to respect and love; when she consented to trust her happiness to me, and that I was in a position to offer her a home with the prospect of a fair competence. We were married in Lyttelton, and she became a worthy helpmate, unsparing and unselfish in all her endeavours for the welfare of our family; and ably supporting me with her counsel and advice, that has mainly contributed to whatever success it has been my good fortune to have attained.

Shortly after this event a terrific storm broke over Lyttelton ; wrecking about half-a-dozen small craft, and one large brig, the 'Torrington,' which was thrown upon the rocks in the bight formed by Officer's Point, and became a total wreck. Her miscellaneous cargo was mostly saved, but in a very damaged condition; and drapery, haberdashery, groceries, and small goods of every description (as it was the boast of her owner that he had everything on board, from an anchor to a needle), with a plentiful admixture of coal-dust and sea-water, being sold by auction in " small lots to suit purchasers," every housewife in Port took the opportunity of laying in a good stock ; and, for a long time after its occurrence, evidences of the wreck, endowed with the remarkable property of locomotion, were to be met with in the most unexpected places in various parts of the town.

The attractions of the Australian gold-diggings offered a powerful check to the young settlement, occurring as they did so soon after its formation ; not only by withdrawing a great deal of the labour that had cost so much to import, but by raising the cost of all the staple articles of consumption, which at that time had to be imported, made it very trying for all classes.

The whole of the winter and spring months of 1851, the wholesale price of flower was £40 per ton (just quadruple the price it had been in Nelson the previous year), the 4lb. loaf was sold at 1/8, which, at the present time of good wages, would be thought almost a famine price. Under these circumstances, and the glowing accounts of rich funds continually coming to hand, it was not surprising that numbers of the labouring population left for the el dorado, and my baker being among the number I had great difficulty in obtaining another.

It was my custom to visit the bake-house the first thing in the morning to be satisfied that all was as it should be. One morning, on entering it about 7 o'clock, I found, instead of the batch being in the oven, the dough for 200 loaves spread out on the boards, and the oven not fired. The baker was down the beach drinking, so I had to finish the work myself.

A Step Matrimonial. 245

As he had determined to go to the diggings, he was not much concerned at his summary dismissal.

For the next three or four months I had to manage the bread-baking business entirely myself, with some help from a lad who was employed in the shop, baking 200 loaves daily, and 400 on Saturdays.

This, with also having to attend to the general business of the store, I began to find was too much, and I was glad to accept the offer of a party to lease the baking premises (as, at this time, it could be disconnected from the store), which terminated my active connection with it.

At this time there was not a vestige of local government, or any government over which the people could exercise any control, and colonial politics claimed and received a great deal of public attention. Under the existing *régime* it was customary for the government brig to make a periodical round of the settlements, and empty all the coffers, and the settlers had to supplicate the Governor *in formâ pauperis* for a small dole of their own money for some absolutely necessary public work.

The colonial financial arrangements of this period were of such a beneficent and fraternal character that provincialists and political economists of the present day cannot hope to emulate. As an instance, the sum of £3000 was taken upon one occasion from Lyttelton, and expended in constructing a lighthouse at Wellington, though in 1848 or 1849 an extra 1/0 per gallon duty was imposed upon brandy for this special purpose.

Mr. Godley's speech, delivered at a very large public meeting held at Lyttelton, commenting upon Sir G. Grey's "Provincial Councils Ordinance," then before the public, counselling its rejection, was considered a masterpiece of cogent reasoning and eloquence. Being echoed through the colony, it helped materially to determine the fate of the measure, which was universally condemned and rejected.

The Colony was ruled at the time referred to by a Nominee Council, in which the paid officials of the government had seats and a

A Step Matrimonial. 247

majority of votes, and in which the Governor had failed to induce any leading settler to accept a seat. In the Provincial Councils proposed to be constituted, the Governor, still tenacious of power, retained the nominee element to the extent of one-third of the number of seats, and was much surprised and chagrined — after making what he thought almost revolutionary concessions—at its summary rejection.

As Lieutenant-Governor Eyre made no secret of his sympathies being with the settlers in their efforts for constitutional changes, he was made the subject of a remarkable despatch from Sir G. Grey to the Home Government, in which he (Lieutenant-Governor Eyre) was represented as making the government of the country very difficult, and almost denouncing him as inciting to rebellion. Canterbury, for seconding Wellington—it may be supposed in the agitation for a more liberal form of government—also came in for a share of the Governor's strictures.

At a meeting of the Legislative Council in June, 1851, Sir George, with singular want of taste and tact as Governor of the whole Colony, made a fierce attack upon the settlement, and the principle upon which it had been founded. Remembering how despotically he once ruled the country, and resented and impugned the motives of earnest, undaunted opponents, he ought to be congratulated upon his recent conversion, and having become so enthusiastic in championing the political privileges of the people.

CHAPTER XI.

TRULY RURAL.

My own personal matters had ceased to fluctuate, and having reached the " dead level of mediocrity " (it being perhaps considered that they were never above it), I think it will be of more interest to the general reader to continue my observations and remarks upon what was passing around me.

The appointment of Colonel Campbell as Crown Lands Commissioner at Canterbury, was very distasteful to the settlers. He was known to them as a disappointed place-hunter, and an adventurer who had assiduously attended the various meetings of the land purchasers and intending colonists in London, and endavoured to ingratiate himself with the members of the Canterbury Association by promises of large purchases of land. Finding he was not likely to succeed in obtaining the appointment of agent in the new settlement he withdrew in disgust, without having purchased an acre, hurried off to the Colony, and, to the surprise of the resident land purchasers, next turned up as the Governor's representative in Canterbury, in a department that brought him into unpleasant contact with many who had had good reasons for forming unfavourable opinions of his actions and character; a department too of all others most nearly affecting the future of the settlement.

A man with fewer qualifications for discharging, with only ordinary efficiency, the duties required in the department to which he had been appointed, could not have been found. It was shrewdly suspected that his new *rôle* of hostility to the settlement, was his chief recommendation for the appointment to the office.

The manner in which the duties were "performed," the ludicrous, if not illiterate, notices and proclamations issued from time to time, and his assiduous raking up and ridiculous

Truly Rural. 251

defence of Hempleman's claims, are they not chronicled in the pages of the 'Lyttelton Times'? The removal of himself and the entire business of his office to Akaroa, a remote spot in those days of infrequent communication, must have seriously affected the business of the department, besides inflicting untold annoyance and expense upon all having occasion to transact business in connection with the Crown lands of the settlement.

The mischief thus wantonly inflicted upon individuals, and a department, by a capricious subordinate, in spite of all remonstrances, met with no reproof or redress from Sir George Grey, and continued until the Constitution Act swept all such abuses of patronage away. His impotent efforts to form townships to the north and south, in immediate proximity to the boundary of the Canterbury block, and the special inducements offered of freer pastoral regulations (by instructions from the Governor we *must* suppose), were regarded at the time as intended to injure or retard this settlement, by attracting from it labour and capital; and would have probably succeeded had the duty been intrusted to an officer of ordinary capacity.

For a proper understanding of the import of this manœuvre (for I cannot otherwise characterise it), it must be remembered that at that time, as little or no improvement had been effected on the plains, and the special advantages for the high price of land within the block not very apparent to persons in the Colony desirous of purchasing land; a few miles north or south were comparatively unimportant, and the prices of the government land, both town and rural, and the liberal pastoral regulations, presented a strong contrast to the terms of purchase within the block.

It was a continuation of the policy and tactics introduced by Governor Hobson; it remains a singular but well attested fact, that the New Zealand Company's settlements and the Canterbury settlement, had to struggle against the open hostility of a government supposed to be established to promote, cherish, and strengthen the colonization of these Islands; and it was only by the strenuous exertions and patriotic devotion of a determined band of able earnest men, of whom the late Dr. Featherston, Hon. W. Fox, Mr. Fiztherbert, and for a brief period only Mr. Godley, were conspicuous examples, that difficulties almost insuperable were met and overcome, and of the fruits of which we are now in the quiet enjoyment.

When Governor Hobson arrived in New Zealand, he fixed his head quarters and seat of government at such a remote corner of the Islands, that the most frequent communication with it was by way of Sydney. It was not alone the studied neglect, which could have been borne, but the opposition, direct attacks, and mischievous interference, of which the settlers had to complain. The annals of the settlement will testify to the circumstance of a vessel having been specially sent from Auckland to Wellington to attract from it labourers imported by the New Zealand Company at great cost, by the offers of high wages and free passages to Auckland.

When Colonel Wakefield was apprised of the starting of an expedition under the charge of his brother Captain Arthur Wakefield, to found the settlement of Nelson, and was desirous that he (Captain Wakefield) should proceed to the Port Cooper plains, having heard from whalers of a fine extent of level country there, Governor Hobson peremptorily forbade his going south, and limited the choice for the new settlement to the shores of Blind Bay, hence Nelson has always been called "Hobson's Choice." Successive Governors, judging by their acts, appear to have zealously followed the traditions of the office, until the Constitution Act conferred the government of the country upon its inhabitants.

Of Mr. Godley I have little more to add, though much might be written. At the close of 1852 his personal connection with the Canterbury Settlement terminated after two years of indefatigable labour; he had a sure prescience that his mission was accomplished; that the settlement was firmly planted, and possessed all the essential elements of progress, and with the measure of local self-government just then conferred upon the Colony by the Constitution Act, he saw that political freedom achieved for which he had been so long and so zealously striving.

Invaluable as his presence and assistance had been to the settlement (which I have but very feebly glanced at), I cannot help with all due diffidence, hazarding an opinion which I dare say will be deemed very heterodox in this Canterbury Settlement, the scene of his disinterested labours. It is simply that in his brief career of usefulness, his wisdom and judgment were never more conspicuously displayed than in choosing the appropriate time of retiring from a position he had filled with such advantage to the settlement. His commanding intellect, winning eloquence, and administrative ability conferred upon him such a proud pre-eminence, and removed him so far above his contemporaries, that, unconsciously it may have been to himself, his was a personal government of the most pronounced type; a kind of intellectual despotism that unintentionally repressed and stifled all free discussion, because no one felt sufficient confidence or ability in himself to enter the arena. It was not that Canterbury was deficient in capable men. Indeed it was far otherwise. As soon as there was a clear field for action, a band of talented men came to the front, and from that time to the present have filled all the most important offices in the gift of the Colony, with credit and honour to themselves, and to the benefit and advantage of their constituents and country.

What appeared to be wanting at this time was the old British privilege of grumbling; this safety valve of all English communities seemed to be overweighted, and there was a general suspicion that the "Captain" was sitting on it. To continue the metaphor, and in a manner to justify it, I may state that immediately after Mr. Godley's departure, there was a great blow off of steam that had evidently been collecting for some time. Mr. Godley embarked at Lyttelton December 21st, 1852, and on January the 1st, 1853, appeared a curiously worded notice in the 'Lyttelton Times,' convening a public meeting. The notice implied that there had been a tyrannical incarceration of indigent immigrants, which the public were called upon to investigate.

Truly Rural. 257

This notice caused some genuine excitement in Lyttelton, to which the public had long been strangers. People formed in small groups at the street corners, and discussed the points of the special grievance with solemn gravity.

At the appointed time a crowded meeting assembled. Dr. Donald was voted to the chair. After considerable discussion, and as a Yankee would say, some "tarnation tall talk" indulged in, Resolution No. 1, censuring the Canterbury Association, was carried with acclamation, though what the Association had to do with the subject in hand I could not make out; but this did not seem of any consequence, the Association was a distant and to some a mythical sort of body, that could be kicked with impunity; but when No. 2 was proposed, reflecting upon individuals by name and at that time in the settlement, it was gently hinted that it was libellous. The chairman felt his responsibility and declined to put it to the meeting. After this elimination of the most lively and interesting part of the proceedings, the business flagged, and was virtually shelved by the appointment of a

s

committee to investigate and report at a future date. The meeting then separated, and "the subsequent proceedings interested them no more."

As far as I could learn the circumstances were as follows: The Canterbury Association scheme provided for the appropriation of a certain proportion of the proceeds from sale of land to assist emigration, and land purchasers were conceded the privilege of nominating parties for passages in proportion to their land purchases. Some one or two land purchasers, upon the refusal of their labourers to continue in their employment at a lower rate of wages than was ruling, and in some instances to work out the passage money, having construed the cost of passage into a debt due to themselves, had obtained judgments for the amounts in the court, and failing payment had imprisoned the debtors. Not being on the investigation committee, or an original land purchaser, I cannot vouch for the accuracy of the foregoing, I merely give it as told me at the time.

Sir G. Grey's first action on receiving the

Constitution Act was to pigeon-hole it for some months, and in the meantime by proclamation to suddenly reduce the price of all the waste lands of the Colony to 5s. and 10s. per acre. This was considered a very unconstitutional proceeding; as leaving the question of price out of consideration, the new Act vested all control of the waste lands in the General Assembly, so soon as that body was legally constituted. But Sir George, in the most arbitrary exercise of power, delayed for many months taking any steps towards initiating the new order of things, and, when he could delay no longer, proceeded to constitute the Provincial Councils, still postponing the principal section of the Act relating to the General Assembly, in order, it was supposed, that his new land regulations might have time to operate.

A gentleman to whom E. G. Wakefield used to refer as a great constitutional lawyer, proceeded to Wellington and moved the Supreme Court in the matter, and obtained the judgment of the Court, declaring that no legal title could issue to purchasers of land under Sir G. Grey's proclamation; which Sir George regarded not, seeing that Acts of Parliament sometimes received scant courtesy when inimical to his views. As Sir G. Grey's proclamation reducing the price of the waste lands could not affect the land within the Canterbury block, unless the Provincial Council about to be constituted chose to adopt it, in which case there was no doubt the Governor would have confirmed such legislation, there began to be formed a strong party in the settlement, but chiefly in Lyttelton, in favour of cheap land (*i.e.*, the government price). I may notice here parenthetically that at this time there were two or three recent arrivals from Australia, with large sums to their credit at the bank to be invested in land (one was stated to have £26,000 which seemed a fabulous sum in those days), not uninterested in the result of the coming struggle and who quietly watched, and waited.

Mr. J. E. FitzGerald was the first candidate for the office of Superintendent, and Mr. Tancred shortly after entered the lists; but as their opinions were identical upon the land question, it was simply a question of men.

The cheap land party saw their opportunity in the division of their opponents, and put forward Colonel Campbell as their candidate, with a very fair prospect of carrying the election. As there was no "Treating at Elections" Bill in force at that date, or any other restriction as particularly affecting elections, full scope could be given to the most exuberant fancy, which was freely indulged by the Radical party. Other stimulants to excitement were not wanting, as two or three public-houses in Lyttelton were considered to be open houses on the day of election, if not for some days before.

A band of music was improvised and so were some of the instruments; a number of empty oil drums were procured, and sheepskin dexterously fitted over the ends, and if noise was the principal desideratum, I must admit they were a great success.

A local artist, of the sign-painter order of merit, executed a large cartoon in gay colours; it was intended to represent one of the two opposition candidates holding a working man's nose to a grindstone, which the other was assiduously turning. This was fixed upon two long staffs, and carried in the procession in the form of a large banner. The explanation of the grindstone device is as follows:—During the first few months of 1851, ships loaded with emigrants arrived in quick succession, and as the barrack accommodation was not equal to such a rapid influx of people, only a very temporary stay could be allowed. I think it was a fortnight, in which time, houses or other accommodation had to be found. It was the duty of the Immigration Agent (J. E. FitzGerald) to carry out the regulations in force, and the compulsory evictions this involved brought him in unpleasant contact with nearly all the immigrants. It was not to be expected that they would be able to draw any nice distinctions between the office and the officer; hence he acquired a degree of unmerited unpopularity with the working-classes that remained for many years.

To return to the election festivities; processioning was the order of the day. Various emblematic devices were improvised for the occasion. As the price of land was supposed to have some indirect influence upon the price of bread, a large loaf had the motto of cheap land attached to it, while dear land was represented by a very diminutive one, and were carried in procession amid a deafening noise, varied at intervals with the enlivening strains of " Cheer, boys, cheer ! " and other popular tunes with good choruses, making things uncommonly lively in Lyttelton while the demonstration lasted.

I am pleased to record that the whole affair was conducted with great good humour, and honest mirth — there being no drunken rowdyism, notwithstanding the opportunities. The result of the election was accepted as a decisive settlement of the cheap *versus* dear land question ; and the Australian land speculators, before referred to, hastened to make their land purchases just outside the block, ere the Provincial Council should quadruple the price.

There was one amusing episode connected

with this election (though we, Mr. Fitz-Gerald's committee, were grave enough about it at the time) that deserves a passing notice. By the election regulations then in force, the onus of objecting to any one not entitled to vote, remained with the constituency, and a personal service of notice to appear before the Resident Magistrate was required to be made within a certain time preceding an election. Being a member of Fitzgerald's committee, I was cognisant of the fact of about fifteen notices being prepared to serve on the parties not qualified to vote, but whose names were on the roll, and unless objected to could exercise their votes.

After a careful scrutiny of the roll, and anticipating a very close contest, it was considered of the greatest importance that these notices should be served on the parties in good time, as they were all cheaplandites. Judge of our chagrin and dismay, when on proceeding to serve the said notices, the birds had flown. Some generous philanthropist had chartered one of the small coasters belonging to the Port, and invited them to take a cruise

Truly Rural. 265

to Akaroa, when after admiring the beauties of that sylvan retreat, they returned from their lengthened picnic, recruited alike in health and spirits, and, with exultant hilarity, resolved themselves into the noisiest of the processionists.

This acceptance, on the part of the opposition, of the election of a superintendent inimical to their views as being conclusive, showed a singular misapprehension of the political importance and power of the holder of that office, as no attempt was made to revive the question at the subsequent elections of the members of the Provincial Council, with whom the decision and settlement really rested.

During the year 1853 there arrived in the Lyttelton harbour the first steam vessel that had been seen in these waters—if we except the surveying ship Acheron, that was engaged surveying the coast of New Zealand previous to the formation of the settlement. I remember the Acheron was at anchor in the Nelson harbour when we started upon the first trip to the wreck of the cutter in September, 1849, and on our way down the harbour we pulled alongside to put a person on board who had missed the last shore boat to the vessel; the individual referred to is now, and has been for many years, a resident of Christchurch.

When the steamer Ann, Gibbs, master, from Sydney, steamed up the harbour in front of the town with colours flying, great was the excitement and jubilation in our small port. The captain was fêted, a breakfast *à la fourchette* (so the tickets styled it) was laid in one of the immigration barracks, and nearly all Port assembled to do honour to the occasion. Champagne corks were flying, and toasts loyal, patriotic, mercantile, and social, were drunk in bumpers, and the most convivial hilarity prevailed.

The captain having brought down an old worn-out river boat, which he was anxious to sell, must have thought he had fallen amongst a singularly primitive and unsophisticated lot of people, and there is no doubt anticipated a speedy and successful termination of his venture. There is no doubt this would have been the case had not the Lyttcltonians (perhaps fortunately in this instance) been in such a very impecunious condition, that they were reluctantly obliged to forego the tempting bait, to the great disappointment of the captain, doubtless, who having risked his life by the voyage from Sydney, had no desire to return thither in the same old tub.

About the latter part of 1854, my wife's failing health induced me to consider the propriety of retiring from the store, and removing to the country away from the ceaseless worry and turmoil of business. Accordingly, by the end of the year all arrangements connected with the disposal of the business having been completed, we took passage with our two children in the Nelson steamer, it being the last trip of that vessel between the settlements on the coast of New Zealand.

The New Zealand Company had reserved a sum of money from the proceeds of land sales, to be devoted to the encouragement and assistance of steam navigation, and the appearance of the Nelson steamer on the coast was due in some measure to the existence of this reserve fund. She was on the coast nearly twelve months, being subsidized, each province paying a proportionate share; but even with this assistance, there was so little intercommunication between the settlements at that time, that after a brief experience she was withdrawn, to the great regret of every one.

Our destination was the Riwaka Valley, where I hoped my wife in the society of her relations and friends, and a pleasant country home, would soon regain her former good state of health. This spot, besides having great natural beauties, had peculiar charms for me, from having been the scene of my early struggles and endeavours. I also felt a pardonable pride in returning to the old neighbourhood, under such improved circumstances after a few years' absence.

I bought a 50-acre section of land for £300, a pair of working bullocks, plough, cart, etc., etc.; indeed, all that was found requisite for a little amateur farming, as I had no idea of being idle; it was simply a change of work, and to me of a most agreeable kind.

I planned a large house, and as I was fond

of carpentry, and not limited to time, I resolved to execute all the work myself; which, with occasional interruptions, occupied about twelve months, including the glazing, paperhanging, and painting, even to the slating the roof, having to send to Lyttelton for the slates, as there were none in Nelson at the time I required them. A neighbour, a slater by trade, specially favoured me, by giving me one day's labour in setting out the work, and instructions how to proceed, etc., and kindly lent me his tools.

With the exception that I probably broke more slates than a professional would have done, I managed it pretty well, and the slater said I had made a very good job of it. I built myself a workshop in which I could do small jobs of carpentry, when the weather did not permit of outdoor work.

There was a school in the neighbourhood, under the charge of a very efficient teacher, which my children, as they successively arrived at school age, attended, and made good progress.

During part of this rustic period, I was

sorely exercised by the rapidity with which my boys' boots became resolved into mere fragments of bad leather; they, one month only, remaining fairly tidy, followed by a week or two of dilapidation, and then discarded for a new pair, which very soon ran the same course. I was remarking one day to the schoolmaster how difficult it was to keep the boys well shod, as the shop boots wore so badly, when he replied, " Why not make them yourself? I make mine and the boy's, and they last four times as long as the shop boots." Upon this it was arranged that I should spend a week of evenings with him, to be initiated into the mysteries of boot-making ; after which I procured the few necessary tools and materials, and there was no further trouble of the boot question during the remainder of my residence in the Riwaka.

Here I lived nine very pleasant, uneventful, happy years ; my wife's health, though never thoroughly re-established, was much improved, the occupation suited me, and was just the kind of life I most preferred. As a resident I gave such time as I could spare to various small public duties, as member of school committee, road board, public library, etc., and had the honour of receiving a deputation upon one occasion, requesting me to allow myself to be nominated for a seat there vacant, to represent the Motueka and Riwaka District in the Nelson Provincial Council; and although I was flattered by the assurance that there would be no opposing candidate, I felt obliged to decline the honour, not feeling sufficient confidence in my ability to fulfil the duties to the satisfaction of myself and constituency. There was a Rifle Volunteer Company at Motueka, and I and several other residents of the valley joined it, and made a point of walking to that place every Saturday to attend drill. Upon one occasion when attending target practice, at the rifle range near the sea beach, Motueka, some of the firing party, while waiting their turn at the target, amused themselves by firing at a supposed log of wood far away on the Moutere flats, where there is shallow water for a considerable distance from shore at that part of Blind Bay. There was a good deal of speculation as to the supposed distance, and the rifle sights were altered and adjusted for various ranges ; each one protesting he was right, and his ball striking the object, or falling very near it. The following day an old Maori Waihinè lodged a complaint at the Resident Magistrate's Court, Motueka, that she had been fired at by the Pakehas while collecting cockles on the mud flat the previous day.

Fortunately for the Maori and Pakeha, there had not been much "judging distance practice" previous to this affair, or the result might have been more serious.

CHAPTER XII.

IN HARNESS AGAIN.

WITH the increase of my family, and the necessity that would soon arise for the two elder boys to leave home to learn some trade or profession, it became a subject for serious consideration between my wife and myself, whether it would not be the most judicious course to pursue to enter once more into, and establish a business, of which the boys could learn the routine, and eventually manage, and continue on their own account. Having decided upon this course and deeming it advisable to carry it into execution without delay, I naturally directed my attention to Canterbury as being the province where there appeared to be the best prospect of succeeding in this object.

T

Accordingly in July, 1863, I visited Christchurch; Canterbury was in an ecstasy of excitement at the time, celebrating the news of the Prince of Wales' marriage; the main streets had not then been macadamised, and as there had been a great deal of wet weather, and road-scrapers unknown, or comparatively useless at that time, they were in a frightfully muddy condition.

I could not help pitying the state of the 600 school children taking part in the procession on the 10th July—all nicely dressed, having to trudge through liquid mud over their boots, throughout the entire route of the procession to the east belt, where the memorial oak was planted.

I succeeded in the object of my visit, as I had not been many days in Christchurch when arrangements were completed for the transfer of an old-established business that I understood, and considered myself competent to manage; I paid a deposit of £600, and was to take possession on the 1st January, 1864.

On my return to the Riwaka, active preparations were begun at once for the projected removal.

In Harness Again. 275

The cutter Nautilus was just taking on board, from the Riwaka Jetty, the last load of black birch timber for the Waiau Bridge, having to deliver the same at Salt-water Creek. As she was a suitably sized craft for crossing the Sumner bar, I chartered her to convey my goods, etc., from the Riwaka Jetty to the Christchurch Quay, after her return from the South.

Having made this opportune arrangement, I decided to take down the house in such a manner that it could be re-erected at Christchurch without much trouble or expense. This was accordingly done, and the materials and other goods were ready for carting to the jetty, when news was received of the cutter having been wrecked in Palliser bay on her return from the South. I was, therefore, under the necessity of having everything conveyed to Nelson by boat; and as the house material was very bulky, and knowing the difficulties and expense of various removals that it was now impossible to avoid, I decided to sell it for what it would fetch on the Nelson Wharf. A purchaser was found for it for £25.

At the appointed time the transfer of the

business was effected, and I entered upon the duties and responsibilities of my new venture with no misgivings for its future, but with some feelings of regret in resigning the comparative freedom and enjoyment of a country life.

At the time here indicated, a period of great activity and prosperity was just coming to a close. I perceived a change was impending; and could I have foreseen the very bad times that ensued, I should have hesitated about choosing that particular time for making a fresh start.

The Australian gold-diggings at first injuriously affected the settlement, but when corn and wool began to be exported, Canterbury, in common with the older provinces, derived the full advantage of the good markets and enhanced prices that resulted. The Otago gold-fields were also of material advantage to its sister province. But now a reaction was about to set in, as experience has shown so frequently occurs after a period of prosperity in the colonies.

It proved of unusual severity and duration; there was a general stagnation and depression in all branches of business; it was not limited

In Harness Again. 277

to New Zealand, but extended over all the Australian Colonies and England, as it was in 1866, when some of the largest London Houses collapsed, bringing ruin upon many smaller ones.

New Zealand had its full share of the bad times that ensued, with its Maori war, and waste of three millions in the endeavour to " Conquer a Peace."

Canterbury, and all the provinces except Auckland (where a large war expenditure maintained a temporary fictitious prosperity), had to pass through a very trying ordeal, that lasted for five or six years; in fact, the tide had just turned when the " Public Works Policy," as it was termed, of 1870, was introduced. And although Canterbury derived as much benefit as any of the other provinces, in the large public expenditure, and revival of immigration that followed, the revival of trade and general prosperity that ensued was not entirely due to this cause. The great advance in value of her staple export, wool, would have alone ensured it, had no loan expenditure taken placé, and with less chance of another reaction from a sudden exhaustion, or discontinuance of such expenditure.

Notwithstanding the bad times referred to, from 1864 to 1870, I had the good fortune to experience a sure though gradual extension of my business, each year marking an improvement upon the preceding one, so that at the close of 1870 it was more than double the amount of the first year's trade, for which I had reason to be very pleased and thankful.

In October, 1870, occurred the great fire at Lyttelton, when nearly all the business part of the town was reduced to ashes and ruin, my old store being included in the general wreck. On Monday evening, October 24th, I, in company with several others, had our attention attracted by a strong glare of fire appearing over the hills in the direction of Lyttelton. We concluded that there was a large fire there, and knowing they had only one small hand engine in the place, we immediately proceeded to the telegraph office, but being after hours, and no one residing on the premises at that time, I at once made for the lodgings of the chief telegraphist, and induced him to get up (for he had retired for the night), and go to the office and try to communicate with Lyttelton.

By this time a number of people had collected, including several firemen in uniform, in front of the office, impressed with the same belief as ourselves. After an interval of about ten minutes, during which the telegraphist had been trying to get communication with the Port without success, he announced from one of the upstair windows, to those below, his opinion that it was only a bush fire on the peninsula. Not sharing this opinion, I rushed to the nearest cab-stand, and was soon conveyed to the foot of the bridle path, where I dismissed the cab and walked to the top of the hill, when I found my forebodings only too truly verified.

The whole of the centre block had been consumed, and its outline was plainly marked by glowing posts standing here and there amid a mass of burning débris, and the fire was then raging chiefly about Canterbury Street, which it appeared to have only just reached. It did not take me long to descend the hill and work my way through back premises and over fences to the rear of my store, as the opposite and adjoining buildings being on fire, there was no access from the street. Part of the stock had been removed to the reclaimed land near the railway, the further removal being stopped by the rapid advance of the fire in the street. As I could do no good by remaining, and the only retreat was by ascending to the top of the bank at the back of the premises, which, being on a level with the ridge of the house, was exposed to the intense heat and dense smoke from the surrounding burning buildings, I considered it prudent to beat a hasty retreat to avoid being caught in a trap as it were. Casting a rapid glance round the shop for something valuable, that could be conveniently carried, I with my load rushed up the steps at the back, and in a stooping posture, across the top of the bank, and had not proceeded far when the whole building was in a mass of flame.

I had just reached the reclaimed land and deposited my waif, when the train arrived bringing the Ch. Ch. Fire Brigade and engine. It appeared that after I left, communication was had with Lyttelton, and in an incredibly short time a train was got ready, and the brigade and engines despatched to the scene of danger. The Lyttelton telegraphist had been vainly trying for Ch. Ch. for about an hour, and then finding it useless, left the office to save some of his effects from his doomed house. Shortly after he was summoned back to the office to save the instruments, as the office had caught fire, but before disconnecting the wire he made one last attempt, and the Ch. Ch. clerk was descending the stairs, when arrested by the Lyttelton signal. A supply of water was soon obtained and the further spread of the fire arrested at my premises, they being the last consumed.

As nearly all the stores, including the bakers' and butchers' shops, had disappeared, and a great many had lost everything they possessed, a relief committee was organised by the noble exertions of Andrew Duncan, Esq., then Mayor of Christchurch; and by the kind co-operation of his honour, Wm. Rolleston, superintendent, an early train was placed at the service of the committee, and by seven o'clock next morning an abundance of provisions of all kinds were distributed gratis to all requiring them.

CHAPTER XIII.

RETIREMENT.

As my reminiscences draw near the present time, and consequently their conclusion, I may be excused for observing a little more reticence regarding purely personal matters than was observed in the earliest stages.

With this almost involuntary limitation, I cannot help feeling my " occupation gone."

Individuals of the most taciturn dispositions can often be very garrulous upon their own affairs; and forestalling the reader, by placing myself in this category, there remains little more for me to write about. I have no imagination; hard " Gradgrind " facts, that are easy to deal with, have here been simply treated, and with their elimination my "happy dispatch" follows as a matter of course.

I may, therefore, briefly state, that my sons not taking to the business I had so successfully established for them, and having made some judicious investments in 1872. I closed with an eligible opportunity that presented itself for its disposal, and it only remains for me to make a few remarks in a short chapter which will conclude this to me pleasant review of old times, hoping the reader will derive equal pleasure from its perusal.

CHAPTER XIV.

CONCLUDING REMARKS.

WITH the influx of such a large number of immigrants that have arrived in this province the last two or three years, there would be almost of necessity some instances of disappointment and temporary inconvenience, perhaps some little suffering, from not immediately finding suitable and accustomed employment.

I have frequently heard it remarked by new arrivals that they regretted not having emigrated in the earlier days of the settlement, believing that all the prizes and chances of success had been monopolised by the first settlers; pointing for confirmation of this opinion to the easy competence and generally

Concluding Remarks. 285

prosperous positions now enjoyed by almost all of them.

To all entertaining this view I would observe, that with the exception of a few, *very few*, who have made lucky, or perhaps it would be more correct to write judicious speculations in land, the majority have carved out their own fortunes and obtained their present positions by patient industry, sobriety, and unwearying perseverance; and there are the same opportunities, and with the same results, awaiting the exercise of the same qualities now, without the trials and privations peculiar to new settlements, and under which doubtless many, totally unfitted for the roughing of colonial life, succumbed.

Recent arrivals are often surprised and disappointed at finding the provinces exhibiting the advanced civilization, and so many of the characteristics of the old established centres of population to which they have been accustomed, and which having so recently left, with perhaps too sanguine expectations, they can hardly realize the fact of being in a new country, and often wish it exhibited a little less of the old (which perhaps from a bitter experience they had hoped had been left far behind) and more of the new. In the towns they find the various sub-divisions of labour in different branches of industry as obtains in the old country; each trade a nucleus of more or less skilled operatives, and being necessarily on a somewhat limited scale, they are easily overdone; that is, artisans and mechanics often arrive and find no immediate opening for their particular calling, and are apt to think they have made a serious mistake in emigrating. Industry, sobriety, and perseverance, essential as they may be to success, require a field for their exercise, and to ensure this it is needful that a man should possess in addition a certain amount of adaptability, or versatility of resources, and a power of turning to anything that may offer in the shape of honest employment, even if lower than the current wages have to be submitted to, until some fair amount of skill is acquired in the new occupation, which can be at any time relinquished when more congenial and accustomed work offers.

I think it will be conceded that the advice here given has been practically illustrated in the foregoing pages. I may be considered to have been a veritable "Jack of all trades," and I dare say have also proved its converse, of being "master of none;" but I have generally managed to pull through with tolerably fair results, and this I take to be the testing point. Few are aware of their capabilities until they are put to the test; therefore let any one arriving in the colony, and depending upon his own exertions, consider the little word "try" as a talisman, that, if it fail to help him out of all his difficulties, he may rest assured will very materially lessen them.

In giving the foregoing details, and results of thirty-four years' experience in the colony, I venture to hope the example may not be altogether fruitless in encouraging new beginners to persevere, and not to be daunted even if some disappointment is at first experienced in finding some things falling short of the sanguine expectations in which new colonists are so apt to indulge. The broad fact, to be soon tested and proved, will still remain, that here in this new and prosperous country, with its immense natural endowment of yet only partially developed resources, there is ample room for generations to come for honest labour to meet and find its just reward—

"*A fair day's wages for a fair day's work.*"

FINIS.

www.ingramcontent.com/pod-product-compliance
Lightning Source LLC
Chambersburg PA
CBHW032051230426
43672CB00009B/1555